CHRIST AND THE WORLD RELIGIONS

By the same Author:

LITURGY AND DOCTRINE
THE STUDY OF THEOLOGY
THE MAKING OF A CHRISTIAN
GOD'S GRACE IN HISTORY
A QUESTION OF CONSCIENCE

CHRIST AND THE WORLD RELIGIONS

by

Charles Davis

HODDER AND STOUGHTON

290
D261

For Anthony,

In spite of whom this book was written

This Volume incorporates the substance of the
Sir D. Owen Evans Memorial Lectures delivered
at the University College of Wales, Aberystwyth,
during the Session 1969 to 1970

CONTENTS

I

PROBLEMS AND ATTITUDES

I

PROBLEMS AND ATTITUDES

The general problem I want to tackle here is the relation between faith in Jesus Christ and the other religious options still drawing allegiance from men.

I approach this as a theological problem, not as an apologetic task. In other words, I am not setting out to defend an existing position, but to clarify what is initially, at least to myself, unclear. My approach is theological because my starting-point is that of a Christian believer and it is not my immediate purpose to put the truth of the Christian faith in question. I am working as a Christian theologian within the context of the Christian tradition. I am asking as a Christian how, while remaining a Christian, I can make sense of the religious diversity that exists among men. At the same time, I do not think that theology should be closed off from philosophy, which brings all religious convictions under scrutiny. The Christian faith ought not to be shielded from any questions that arise concerning its truth or its claims in an investigation like this. It should in any case be open as in the past to modification from new data and new questioning. If the pursuit of truth is philosophical when its possible results are in no way predicted or limited in advance, then this enquiry is philosophical, although its immediate aim is the understanding and development of the Christian position.

The problem I am raising is to a great extent a new problem both for ordinary Christians and for theologians. Religious diversity now presses upon us in a way it did not before. It has always existed, but it has not affected Christians nor caused much theological concern until recent decades. I will begin this investigation, then, by examining the emergence of religious pluralism as a problem.

If we are far as yet from a world community in the sense of mutual understanding and unity of purpose and action, modern means of communication have already created the beginnings of a global consciousness. People of different countries and cultures live now in mutual awareness, know more and more about one another and are being increasingly brought into personal contact. We no longer live in ignorance of other ways of thinking, other customs and other religions. Men of an earlier age knew vaguely of other religions, but these remained too remote and strange to be taken seriously alongside their own religion. Nowadays, despite persistent claims to distinctiveness, every religion, including Christianity, is classified with other religions as alternative ways of interpreting life. Religious pluralism has entered our consciousness and deprived the Christian religion of its unquestioned monopoly, even when it remains our personal choice.

Admittedly, there is a recessive element in the present world situation; namely, the upsurge in many places of various forms of nationalism and tribalism. But Arnold Toynbee is probably right in seeing as dominant the trend towards the disengagement of religion from hereditary and geographical determinants, so that people make a free choice from several different religions in grown-up life. In *Christianity Among the Religions of the World* he writes:

> Today, I think, we can see the World changing from one in which a man's religion used to be decided for him *a priori* by his birthplace, by the accident of birth, into a world in which, to a greater and greater degree, as the World grows together, he will be able to make a free choice, as an adult, between alternative religions.[1]

The world as a whole is still very far from a free market in religions, but a naïve and untroubled exclusiveness in religion is becoming increasingly difficult to preserve. The growing awareness that other men think and act differently is a factor making for openness and greater personal freedom.

On the scholarly level an accurate, detailed knowledge of religions other than Christianity, of their sacred texts, customs, beliefs, rites and history, was first achieved by the West in the nineteenth century. Before that time knowledge was fragmentary and unreliable. The immense stock of information built up in the nineteenth century and the first decades of this is still being added to and corrected. But what is more notable in the twentieth century is that much of this knowledge has been popularised and has, besides, been given a personal dimension.[2] Everywhere we see paperbacks on the world religions or giving translations of their texts, and these books have a ready sale. The personal dimension comes first from the intermingling of people of different faiths through travel and immigration. Other religions do not exist for us merely in books, but as the faith of people we meet and know. Secondly, the interest in other religions is personal, not just academic, because people are buying and reading the popular books in order to learn from other religions in seeking a personal faith for themselves.

That many people in the West today are engaged in a search for a personal faith is the result of a change in modern society in the social place and function of religion. The German sociologist, Thomas Luckmann, has discussed this change in *The Invisible Religion*.[3] In modern industrial society there is no longer an official interpretative scheme, relating society and its institutions to an overarching and transcendent universe of meaning. Society has become segmented, and the various institutional areas, such as politics and economics, are ordered autonomously by a functional rationality, without reference to a traditional system of ultimate meaning. It is left to the individual to choose his own interpretative scheme or world-view. Systems of ultimate meaning are a matter of consumer preference, and quite a varied assortment is now available. Religion, then, in present Western society belongs to the sphere of individual choice, even if many simply drift with their family or social group instead of exercising a truly personal decision. This, then, is the situation in which other religions are attracting widespread attention in the previously Christian West. And in this situation the plurality of religions has a considerable impact upon the consciousness even of those who remain orthodox Christians.

The growing interest in other religions is linked with a change of position of the West *vis-à-vis* the rest of the world.

Our time has seen the reaction against colonialism and the attempt to shake off the political and economic hegemony of the Western powers. One country after another has gained self-government. How far they have been really successful in ridding themselves of Western control is another matter—but that does not concern us here. What does concern us is the fierce repudiation of any Western claim to cultural superiority. It is true that throughout the world everyone wants to appropriate and profit from the scientific knowledge and technical skill of the West. But, whether we in the West would judge this inconsistent or not, there is an emphatic refusal to admit that the present Western primacy in science and technology implies any general cultural superiority. As far as religion is concerned, which is not as in the West clearly distinguished from other cultural elements, a strong revival has taken place in India, in the Buddhist countries and in Islam. Hinduism has indeed acquired a new understanding of itself as a universal religion with a universal mission, a self-understanding it did not have before.

There has been a great change from the nineteenth century to the present in the attitude to Christianity. In the nineteenth century the great Eastern religions were on the defensive in relation to Christians and their claims. The East had been temporarily overwhelmed by the rise of the West with its confident sense of superiority, its energy and purpose, its power. However unwelcome, a sense of social backwardness was created, and this prompted a desire for reform to meet the harsh but sometimes justifiable criticisms of the Westerners. In that setting there was little inclination openly to challenge the claim made by missionaries of moral and religious superiority for the Christian religion.

On the contrary, as there were those who were attracted by Western humanist values, so there were some early reformers who spoke with admiration of Christ and his teaching. A very different outlook prevails today. Not only is any Christian title to superiority rejected, but its inferiority is proclaimed. Hindu and Buddhist writers are eager to show how their religion is free from the defects of Christianity and for that reason, unlike Christianity, able to offer a remedy for the present ills of mankind.

This resurgence of the Eastern religions has coincided with a loss of confidence by the West in its own cultural values and with the diminishing place of Christianity in Western society and culture. Many sensitive people in the West have a guilty conscience about Western imperialism and economic exploitation. They feel a spiritual emptiness in Western civilisation. They have no inclination to boast about a supposed Western superiority. Meanwhile, the decline of the Christian faith in an increasingly post-Christian society leaves Christians themselves on the defensive, without the self-assurance of previous generations. There is indeed considerable disagreement in assessing, whether sociologically or ideologically, the so-called secularisation of the West. But at least it must be said that traditional Christianity no longer draws unquestioned allegiance and that the present religious situation is a somewhat confused medley of competing options.

New religious vitality and assurance in the East and religious confusion and loss of confidence in the West: this is the setting for what Hendrik Kraemer has called the "Eastern Invasion" of the West.[4] Ironically, this invasion has been brought about chiefly by the West itself. It was Western scholars who gave the East a new awareness of its religious heritage and a fresh knowledge of its ancient texts. Western invitations and eagerness have so far been the chief stimulus of Hindu and Buddhist missionary activity in the West. It has been Western writers and devotees who have popularised Eastern religions for a wide reading public. While the Eastern presence in the West is undeniable, the extent of its impact is impossible to assess. As Kraemer writes:

2

The fact remains that the peculiar spirit, the dynamic, the motive forces and the achievements of the great Eastern cultures, religions and philosophies occupy a place, play a rôle, co-determine the chaotic multilogue in which the Western world finds itself, groping in the dark towards an undefined and indefinable new unity of life. Nobody can tell exactly how far this occupying a place, this playing a rôle, goes. We have no methods or instruments for measuring it. But the fact is there.[5]

The admiration of the West for Eastern culture goes back to the eighteenth century and the uncritical praise of all things Chinese during the period of the Enlightenment. Then, too, began the tradition of using Eastern culture as a stick with which to beat the Christian culture of the West for its failings. In Germany the Schlegel brothers were pioneers in promoting an interest in the East. One of them, Friedrich, published *The Language and Wisdom of the Hindus* in 1808, a book which is said to have had a profound influence upon the German Romantic Movement. But a more important place in the history of Eastern thought in the West is usually given to Schopenhauer (1788–1860), who on a very inadequate textual basis lauded the wisdom of the Upanishads and used it as a standard for judging Christianity. The latter half of the nineteenth century saw the work of the Orientalists, notably Max Müller, in editing and translating sacred texts. On the popular level, Sir Edwin Arnold's long poem, *Light of Asia*, published in 1879, made many familiar with the Buddha and his teaching. At the end of the nineteenth century, in 1893, a World Parliament of Religions was held in connexion with the Chicago World Fair. There, in a speech that made a tremendous impact, the young Vivekananda, presented Hinduism as a universal faith for mankind. A few years later, in 1897, he founded the Ramakrishna Mission, named after the famous Hindu holy man whose disciple he had been. The Ramakrishna Mission, which may be taken as representing a newly awakened Hinduism, propagates the mystical monism of the Vedanta in the West and active social concern in India itself. As for the twentieth century, the indications are that interest as well as knowledge of Eastern religions has increased. The Vedanta has attracted distinguished adherents, such as Christopher Isherwood and Aldous Huxley. There are many Buddhist groups in the West and, in particular, Zen Buddhism retains the vogue first given to it by Professor Suzuki. And perhaps it is not too incongruous to mention as symptoms of the condition of the West that the Beatles sit at the feet of a Hindu guru, some Christians are practising yoga, and Malcolm X turned to Islam and found there a sense of the equality of all races that put white Christians to shame.

My remarks about the influence of Eastern religions have been fragmentary and impressionistic. But even though a more adequate account of this could be given, there is, as I have already said, no way of precisely determining its extent. A more useful question is whether there are any grounds for supposing that the religions of the East can provide the spiritual resources the West would seem to need and be looking for at the present time. But there is no clear answer to that question either. Devotees of Eastern wisdom unhesitatingly answer yes, and some Christians give an equally ready no. Those with less firm presuppositions than these two groups find the whole matter of possible interaction between East and West more complicated and uncertain.

Much of the difficulty lies in determining the relationship between the Christian religion and the secular dynamic of the West. By the secular dynamic I mean the concern with this world, the thrust towards the mastery of nature and control of human life and development, which produced the scientific and technological revolutions and has so amazingly transformed the conditions of human existence.

Whatever may be said in theory about the compatibility between this secular dynamic and religion, it would seem in fact to have been inimical to traditional religion. In the West society after the technological revolution is no longer Christian and the various institutional areas of society have thrown off any subordination to religious symbols or religious authority. The emergence of modern society has been accompanied by secularism, which means the rejection of the transcendent or sacred, and by widespread religious indifference.

Nevertheless, there are some recent Christian writers—they have been named secular theologians—who have maintained that appearances in this matter are deceptive. Distinguishing between secularisation as a process and secularism as a closed ideology, they welcome secularisation as the liberation of the secular and the historical from a sacred wrongly conceived as a static sacral order. They further argue that the secularising process has its origins in the biblical tradition. The distinctive emphasis this gives to the transcendence of God resulted in a desacralising of the world. Further, there was the importance given to history in biblical religion. A secular world and a sense of ongoing history are the twin causes of secularisation. The secular dynamic of the West is thus for them a Christian product, and Christian, too, is its opposition to religion, at least when religion is understood as the dominance of a traditional and unchanging sacred or other-worldly order. The secular theologians, however, differ among themselves in interpreting religion and the transcendent.

A writer who has applied what may be called the thesis of Christian secularity to the question of the attitude of the West to the religions of the East is Van Leeuwen in *Christianity in World History: The Meeting of the Faiths of East and West*.[6] For him the secular culture of the modern West is the fruit and authentic manifestation in human history of the Christian revelation. Religion is a past cultural form. He writes:

All religions—Christianity included—have had a structural affinity to the Neolithic era; and by that is meant the era of agricultural-cum-pastoral societies, for which the Neolithic revolution provided a basis and the major primary civilisations the characteristic patterns. The Neolithic era was that in which societies were—and were bound to be—unconditionally religious. It is that form of society which the modern techno-logical revolution has transformed, quintessentially and for the first time. The position of Christianity in respect to this revolution is an extraordinary one, precisely because Christianity was responsible for bringing it about. As the revolution spreads to other societies, so there—just as in the West—it augurs the beginning of the end for the Neolithic era.[7]

The secular West, so the argument continues, is now breaking up the traditional religious cultures of the East through the extension of the modern technological revolution over the whole world. The spread of secularisation, together with the disintegration of religious cultures it brings, is a matter for rejoicing. It is the way in which Christianity is beginning to exercise a universal function. Christians should not concern themselves with solving the problems raised by other religions with the help of the Christian religion, but rather help adherents of other religions to cast off the bondage of a religious world view and enter the freedom of a secular world.

That interpretation of the secular dynamic of the West implies a negative attitude to the Eastern religions and indeed to all the features of Christianity that bring it under the category of religion. It certainly does not see the East as providing new spiritual resources for the West.

"A latter-day manifestation of the cultural tribalism of the West" is how Ninian Smart dubs the Christian secularity thesis, though he is directly referring to another secular theologian, Paul van Buren, not Van Leeuwen. It is a fallacy, he argues, to identify civilisation with Europe and America and to think of history as constituted by Western history. Even in the West secularism is not universal. "Further afield, Islam, Hinduism and Buddhism retain vast energies. It is nonsense to think of the world as essentially alienated from religion and ideology; and it is doubtful, to say the least, that non-Western cultures will have a Western future . . . There is no strong rational basis for supposing that the world-wide ripples of technology will turn men away from their traditional religious and ideological beliefs."[8] Therefore Ninian Smart, as his other writings also show,[9] considers a dialogue between the faiths of East and West to be mutually of value.

It is possible to share Ninian Smart's impatience with the extreme version of Christian secularity and yet feel that he underplays the problem raised for all religions by modern secularism. Paul Tillich, who was not uncritical of secular man's bid for autonomy, saw secularism as a key factor in the present encounter of world religions. As he puts it in his booklet, *Christianity and the Encounter of the World Religions*:

> . . . the main characteristic of the present encounter of the world religions is their encounter with the quasi-religions of our time. Even the mutual relations of the religions proper are decisively influenced by the encounter of each of them with secularism, and one or more of the quasi-religions which are based upon secularism.[10]

And towards the end of his analysis he ventures "the idea that the secularisation of the main groups of present-day mankind may be the way to their religious transformation".[11]

What this means is that the future shape and role of the Eastern religions will be determined by the outcome of their encounter with secular dynamic of the West, and with the quasi-religions, such as nationalism, Communism, secularist humanism, derived from it. There is no need to suppose a Western future for the East in order to admit a transformation of the East under the impact of the West. The Indian scholar and statesman, K. M. Panikkar, considers that the period of Western dominance of Asia, which he calls the Vasco da Gama epoch, now at an end, has undeniably brought about a qualitative break with the past. To quote:

> Though it is impossible to anticipate what Asia will make of these influences in the future, and how the different Asian countries will transmute the experiences, ideas and institutions in the crucible of their racial characteristics, history and social tradition, there is no gainsaying the fact that the massiveness of the changes that have already taken place, the upsurges which

have radically transformed their ancient societies, and the ideas that have modified their outlook, involve a qualitative break with the past which justly entitles the changes to be described as revolutionary.[12]

At the same time, he maintains that the missionary attempt to convert Asia has "definitely failed"[13] and indeed left Hinduism, Buddhism and Islam "stronger and more vigorous as a result of the adjustments they were called upon to effect".[14] But the fact that these religions are stronger today

> does not mean that they have not undergone profound changes. As against other religions and other philosophies they have more than held their own; but they have also had to undergo subtle transformations to resolve the conflicts which modern science, more than rival religions, forced on them. Thus the new interpretations of Buddhism and Hinduism reflect in a large measure the influence of modern ideas, mostly arising from contact with Europe.[15]

In other words, granted the continued identity and vitality of the Asian civilisations and religions, it can still be argued that what chiefly determines their present situation and future development is the impact of the secular dynamic originating in the West.

This puts the Eastern religions in a similar situation to Christianity. All the religions share the common problem of relating their religious concern to the secular forces and interests of modern society. Which brings us back to the question whether the Christian West can expect light from the East in meeting the problem of secularism, with which it has so long struggled but which is now so deeply affecting the religions of the East.

Geoffrey Parrinder has written a book, *The Christian Debate: Light from the East*,[16] to show how Christians might look to the East in grappling with present problems. He sees the coming of Eastern teachings to the West as a third Reformation, following upon the first in the sixteenth century and the second in the nine-teenth century with the impact of the scientific revolution.[17] David Edwards, on the contrary, does not find the appeal to the East at all convincing. In *Religion and Change*[18] he argues first that the doctrinal content of the religion of the East in the future may well be based on the ultimacy of man rather than on belief in the supernatural. In which case there is no need for the West to learn this. It has a vigorous home-grown secularism. Secondly, contrasting the static character of the East with the dynamic energy of the West, which it derived chiefly from its religion, he concludes: "the spiritual legacy of Christianity, Judaism and Islam did much to inspire the scientific civilisation; and it is diffi-cult to imagine that the dynamism will be inspired in the future by the religion of the East".[19] The future of the whole world thus largely depends, according to Edwards, upon what the West makes of its own religious tradition.

Although Arnold Toynbee works with a narrower concept of the West than David Edwards, he would, I think, grant a greater part to the East in determining the future of Western civilisation and of the world as a whole. In *Civilization on Trial* he envisages future historians looking back upon the past: in A.D. 2047 they will see the impact of Western civilisation upon all the other living societies of the world as the great event of the twentieth century; in A.D. 3047 they will be chiefly interested in the tre-mendous counter-effects from these societies, from Orthodox Christendom, from Islam, from Hinduism, from the Far East, which may have transformed Western civilisation almost beyond recognition; by A.D. 4047 the distinction between Western civilisation and the other civilisations will probably seem unim-portant, with the unity of mankind by then a fundamental con-dition of human life; and, finally, the historians of A.D. 5047 will regard religion as the key factor in that social unification.[20]

Predicting the future is a fascinating but perilous business. Since both West and East are in the midst of profound changes, it would seem unwise to limit from either side the possible out-come of interaction. The remark is banal; but both those who, proclaiming Christianity effete, extol the wisdom of the East and those who, enamoured of Western technology and secular freedom, dismiss the East as static and backward are closing off a dialogue that has hardly as yet begun. Most writers avoid those extremes, but there is a tendency to want to measure the abundance or paucity of fruits in advance, whereas the labour of garnering them must come first.

The future outcome of the interaction between the religions of the East and the Christian and post-Christian West is thus still uncertain and open to differing assessments. But interaction there will be, and dialogue among the religions is becoming unavoidable. Increasingly it is difficult to raise any religious question among young people without discussing it against the background of all the world religions. The general experience of the departments of religion in North American universities is that the young are keenly interested in religious questions. The departments are flourishing and the enrolment is high. But the students do not want these questions to be handled within a Christian framework of ideas. Even where there is no special enthusiasm for Eastern religions nor any disillusionment with the Christian faith, they still want to know what religions other than Christianity say. They wish questions to be discussed with reference to the total religious tradition of mankind. Religious pluralism has undoubtedly entered into the consciousness of the younger generation. Dr Trevor Ling notes a similar development among English sixth-formers.[21]

This, then, is the setting for any investigation into the relation between Christ and the world religions. Christians are now living in a world where adherents of different religions freely intermingle, work together and sometimes enter into friendship. They find themselves in a situation where increasingly account must be taken of other religions and where these religions are attracting many in the once exclusively Christian West. Part of an intelligent Christian faith today must be the acknowledgement that other men, intelligent and sincere, hold other faiths. Inherent in any faith that is not lived in ignorance or turned into prejudice is an awareness of religious plurality and respect for the faith of other men. But this awareness inevitably leads to reflection upon the problem religious diversity raises for Christianity with its traditional belief in Christ as the final revelation of God and universal Saviour of men. The Christian has to grapple with the existence and value of other religions and account for this religious plurality theologically if in the present situation he is to clarify both his faith in Christ and his practical attitude towards other religions and their adherents.

I have been giving reasons to explain why religious diversity, which has always been a fact, has become a problem pressing upon the Christian believer and calling for attention from the Christian theologian. In setting forth the state of the question I want now to bring out into the open a factor that makes the whole question a tricky one for the Christian theologian: namely, the *a priori* hostility towards any religious claim to universal truth, uniqueness, finality or exclusiveness, particularly such a claim on the part of Christianity. I have multiplied expressions because the chief purpose of this investigation is to clarify in which sense, if any, the Christian faith is final or exclusive, and I do not wish to determine this beforehand. But everyone is aware that Christians have claimed their faith to be in some sense supreme and final as compared with other faiths. As a matter of fact, they are not alone in making such a claim: Islam and Theravada Buddhism, to mention no others, are similarly exclusive. But the spontaneous rejection of a religious claim to exclusive truth is more noticeable, and indeed more vehement, in the case of Christianity. What are the reasons for the *a priori* refusal to countenance a claim to supreme and final religious truth?

Relativism in religious matters is now so widespread and so much taken for granted that even to ask reasons for it seems naïve. But it would distort the present discussion and even in fact render it pointless were we to dismiss every absolute religious claim without a hearing.

It is necessary to distinguish the Christian faith in Christ as the one Saviour and embodiment of final truth from its parasite: the arrogance of the Christian West. However much a sense of personal and cultural superiority has motivated and marred Christian missions, it is not an essential feature of the Christian claim nor its necessary consequence. Far from this, the assumption of superiority by Christians contradicts the Christian faith itself with its insistence upon salvation as God's gratuitous gift or grace, not man's achievement. As Hendrik Kraemer, the noted proponent of Christian exclusiveness, points out: "The feeling of superiority is essentially a cultural, and not at all a religious, product; and decidedly not a Christian one. A feeling of superiority can only thrive on a definite consciousness of achievement."[22] And he goes on to observe with some acuteness that when the absolute claim made by Christians is dropped the attempt of some liberals, such as Troeltsch, to keep Christianity relatively supreme as the highest spiritual attainment among the historical religions becomes an unjustified expression of cultural superiority. In his own words:

> The famous student of religion, Troeltsch, who declined the Christian claim of representing the ultimate, exclusive truth as revealed in Jesus Christ, yet who nevertheless maintained a so-called relative absoluteness for Christianity, was virtually giving expression to his innate feeling of Western cultural achievement. There is no reason why a Hindu or a Chinese, being nurtured in his particular atmosphere, should not claim, after a comparative survey of the cultures and religions of the world, the same relative absoluteness with regard to his religion.[23]

Belief in a transcendent revelation, if consistently held, does not imply any personal or cultural superiority on the part of its recipients. As transcendent the revelation relativises all human achievement, including that achievement bound up with or consequent upon its reception. It can and should be announced to others with the conviction that their reception and formulation of it will be of equal validity with that of its present bearers. On the other hand, any attempt to place Christianity first in a hierarchy of religions without making any absolute claim for its particular revelation is, however gently expressed, a manifestation of cultural arrogance.

Undeniably there are difficulties in maintaining the traditional Christian faith in Jesus Christ as the one, universal Saviour and definitive revelation of God to men. Some of these difficulties arise from within the Christian faith itself, such as the difficulty of reconciling the historical particularity of Jesus with God's offer of salvation to all men. Other difficulties are due to the growing intellectual and emotional impact of a pluralist situation. But granted the difficulties, there would not seem to be any inherent contradiction within a religious framework in holding that a particular revelation embodied the highest truth in a definitive fashion for all men. There is point, then, in asking why such a conviction should seem so repugnant to many today and be dismissed as a mere sign of religious prejudice or the mark of a closed mind, even when Western arrogance is not an important influence in provoking a negative response.

In handling this question the German theologian, Joseph Ratzinger,[24] finds two elements in modern man's idea of religion. That idea is both static and symbolic.

The static element is manifest in the negative attitude towards conversion, that is towards any change from one religion to another, together with a reserved and suspicious attitude to missionary activity or proselytism. Each man should remain within the religious tradition in which he was brought up and to which he culturally belongs, unless there are exceptional and compelling reasons to the contrary.

I think a comment is called for here before going on to Fr Ratzinger's second element. The static concept of religion he describes is clearly incompatible with the recent developments I have previously outlined, namely, the move from a cultural to a genuinely personal faith and the growing interest of the West in Eastern religions. Nevertheless, he is right, I think, in seeing a static concept of religion as a factor in the present situation. Part of our present confusion is the intermingling of inconsistent elements.

On the popular level the static understanding of religion chiefly takes the form of a dislike of Christian proselytism and a feeling that Christians should cease their attempts to change the religion of others. The same dislike is not usually extended to Hindu and Buddhist missionary efforts. However, from various quarters the conviction that one should remain within one's own religious tradition finds intellectual formulation from time to time, even omitting consideration for the moment of its pre-eminent expression in modern Hindu thought. A striking recent example is given us by Richard Rubenstein, the Jewish theologian. Rejecting faith in the God of history as no longer possible after Auschwitz and the murder of six million Jews, he wants to retain religion as "the way in which we share and celebrate, both consciously and unconsciously, through the inherited myths, rituals, and traditions of our communities, the dilemmas and the crises of life and death, good and evil".[25]

To understand religion in that way is to acknowledge its givenness. Each of us is "thrown into" his religious situation, which, in a certain sense, is beyond choice.

We can choose the relative degree to which we take seriously our inherited religious traditions. We can, if we want, deny them, but this denial will be dialectically related to the original fact of the givenness of our traditions. Our religious affirmations are very largely the ratification of what is given and the making explicit of what is originally implicit in our situations. Nevertheless, the more serious we become about the domain of that which Paul Tillich calls "ultimate concern", the more we find that we must utilise the sacred forms and traditions of the communities into which we have been thrust.[26]

A similar, though usually less sceptical, stance is sometimes taken by Christians to justify their continued adherence to a particular Church when they no longer accept its distinctive doctrines.

The attitude which views religion as inherited and rejects changing from one religion to another is a strong reminder of the cultural involvement of every concrete religion, and that is part of our present problem. But the presupposition of the attitude would seem to be that all religions are identical in their religious core, or at least—to put it from a more agnostic standpoint— serve the same religious function, so that it is always unnecessary and undesirable to step outside one's cultural background in seeking religious truth. This brings me back to Fr Ratzinger and the second element he discerns in the modern idea of religion: the symbolic element.

According to this, religion in all its expressions is of the symbolic order. Further, so the conviction goes, underlying the many variations and combinations of particular symbols is a fundamental unity of pattern and of meaning, proper to the symbolic order or universe of symbols to which religion belongs. This sense of ultimate unity beneath symbolic diversity is seemingly confirmed by depth psychology, especially in its Jungian form. Jung appealed to archetypes to account for the recurrence, under superficially diverse forms, of primordial images. Likewise, it is argued, the history of religions has uncovered similar patterns emerging in diverse expressions in different religions.

In brief, the contrast between religious and scientific talk is now widely felt and insisted upon. As a consequence religion in its expressions is generally placed under symbolism. And from that arises the widespread conviction that, despite variations of symbolic expression, all religions are in effect saying the same thing.

Now, as many will have immediately noticed, and as Ratzinger himself observes, what he has analysed as the modern idea of religion corresponds to the Hindu view, at least in so far as that view is represented by modern Hindu apologists, notably Radhakrishnan.[27]

Mahatma Gandhi, it will be remembered, insisted upon *swadeshi*, namely that each man should keep to his own religion, and strongly opposed conversions or proselytism. Radhakrishnan on his part denounces the destructive effects of removing people from their ancestral religion:

If we tear up the individual from his traditional roots he becomes abstract and aberrant. Those who believe in conversion
look upon the historical process as a tyranny imposed on man
from without, and assume that the choice of a religion is made
by a process not different from spinning a coin. History is
something organic, a phase of man's terrestrial destiny as
essential for him as memory is for personal identity. It is the
triumph of memory over the spirit of corruption. To forget our
social past is to forget our descent.[28]

He maintains that Hinduism is pre-eminent in showing respect
for each man's religion and in understanding the laws of religious
growth. This is because the Hindu view is tolerant and undog-
matic. It acknowledges value in all religious convictions and
practices, understanding them all as various approaches to God.
Hinduism, he writes:

> does not distinguish ideas of God as true and false, adopting
> one particular idea as the standard for the whole human race.
> It accepts the obvious fact that mankind seeks its goal of God
> at various levels and in various directions, and feels sympathy
> with every stage of the search.[29]

This is not a negative tolerance. The different cults are brought
into mutually helpful relations and arranged according to the
different levels of truth and goodness they represent.

Hinduism accepts all religions as facts and arranges them in
the order of their more or less intrinsic significance. The be-
wildering polytheism of the mass and the uncompromising
monotheism of the classes are for the Hindu the expressions of
one and the same force at different levels. Hinduism insists on
our working steadily upwards and improving our knowledge
of God.[30]

At the highest level are the worshippers of the Absolute, then in the second place come the worshippers of the personal God, and so on down to the worshippers of petty forces and spirits.

The fundamental principle underlying Hindu comprehensiveness is as put in a brief sentence of Radhakrishnan: "The intellectual representations of the religious mystery are relative and symbolic."[31] Or, as he expounds it more fully:

> Toleration is the homage which the finite mind pays to the inexhaustibility of the Infinite.
>
> Only in the experience of the greatest contemplatives do we have the pure apprehension of the Absolute, the utter surrender of the creature to the uncreated spirit. The use of symbols and images is forced on us by our nature. Our thinking and feeling are intimately related to the world of things in which we live. By reference to things that are seen we give concrete form to the intuition of the reality that is unseen. Symbolism is an essential part of human life, the only possible response of a creature conditioned by time and space to the timeless and spaceless reality. Whether we pin our faith to stocks and stones or abstract thoughts and notions we are using concrete symbols which are impoverishments of the Supreme . . . A temporal and finite form of symbolism cannot be regarded as unique, definitive, and absolute.[32]

On this basis religious exclusiveness is vehemently rejected:

> It is not fair to God or man to assume that one people are the chosen of God, that their religion occupies a central place in the religious development of mankind, and that all others should borrow from them or suffer spiritual destitution.[33]

The way to religious unity and peace is to accept "something like the Hindu solution, which seeks the unity of religion not in a common creed but in a common quest".[34] And it is fairly certain, so Radhakrishnan declares, that the Hindu solution of the problem of the conflict of religions is likely to be accepted in the future.[35] He looks forward to a spiritual community uniting the whole human race in the not too distant future:

The time may come sooner than many of us expect when churches, temples and mosques will welcome all men of good will, when faith in God and love of man will be the only requisites for mutual fellowship and service, when the whole of humanity will be bound by one spirit though not by one name.[36]

No longer slaves to words, we shall pass beyond the various names and labels to the life behind them where men can meet in religious unity.

The attitude eloquently defended by Radhakrishnan has a powerful appeal at first impact, and there is little doubt that his outlook is most congenial to a great number of people in the West today. Because of the intrinsic value and interest of Hindu comprehensiveness in its modern form, little is gained theologically by pointing, as the Christian writer, Devanandan, does, to its present political usefulness in India. Noting that any resurgence of Hinduism on the popular level would jeopardise national unity on account of religious diversity within Hinduism itself, he connects the emphasis that all religions are the same with the need to create a national community consciousness. He writes:

What we must not overlook in this development is that this dogma of a religious relativism is proclaimed in India today for two primary reasons; one is that only thereby can Hindus develop a sense of community and national coherence; and the other is that the Indian ideal of a secular state can be founded securely on the belief that all religions, both within and without the larger whole of Hinduism, are the same after all.[37]

There is probably much truth in that; religious relativism does suit the political situation in India at the present time. And,

3

no doubt, the feeling that religious conflict would be avoided and the road towards world community made smoother partially in a similar way explains its attractiveness in the West. But both its theological roots in India and its present congeniality to the West run much deeper than political expediency.

Now, what, I think, should be noted about the Hindu view in its properly religious form is that it is not as tolerant or comprehensive as at first appears. It represents a particular understanding of the nature of religious truth, and this understanding is dogmatically asserted against any other. It consists in taking an inner, formless, mystical experience of the Absolute as alone of ultimate validity, so that all religious statements, all articulate revelations, all formulations, rites, events, authorities, are relative and variable. Nothing is of permanent, absolute authority in religion except the formless, inexpressible experience that underlies the various external forms and symbols of the different religions. In the last analysis ineffable mystical experience is the sole criterion of genuine religion or religious truth.

Opposed to this is the understanding of religious truth characteristic of what Ratzinger calls "revolutionary monotheism", found in Israel, Christianity and Islam. There what is of ultimate validity is not an ineffable mystical experience but the prophetic word apprehended as coming from God. This takes the particular and historical as the decisive criterion because embodying an active communication of a personal God. Obedience to God's word manifest in history rather than absorption into the timeless One is the final criterion of genuine religion.

These two different notions of religious truth raise questions to which I shall have to return later. I may note in passing that the same distinction is made in a less sharp and more eirenic fashion by Ninian Smart in *The Yogi and the Devotee*. He says that there are at least two main ways in which the transcendent is conceived as being revealed or seen in human experience: one is by some earthly manifestation and the other is in religious experience. He provisionally calls these two modes of revelation "mythological revelation" and "experiential revelation". He regards this way of

distinguishing them only provisional because of the close relation
between mythology and religious experience. But a rough-and-
ready line can be drawn "between the concretely conceived
manifestation of the Transcendent through earthly acts, lying,
as it were, in the public domain, and the existentially conceived
visions and inner contemplative states through which the Transcendent can appear to individuals, lying, so to say, in the private
domain".[38] He goes on to point out that religions differ in their
emphasis upon mythological revelation and experiential revelation. Modern Vedanta puts its chief weight upon experiential
revelation, Christianity upon mythological revelation. Later on
he has occasion to observe that Radhakrishnan assumes the
supremacy of the mystical or contemplative experience.[39]

I do not wish to discuss the distinction further at this point. I
merely want to insist that, whether we relate or oppose them,
there are two different approaches to religious truth. It is dis-
ingenuous to demand a prior acceptance of the Hindu view in the
name of tolerance and comprehensiveness. One may legitimately
disagree with the attitude of revolutionary monotheism and with
the decisive place it gives to mythological revelation and urge
arguments against it. What is not legitimate is in the name of
tolerance to demand at the outset that all should accept the mystical understanding of religious truth with the supremacy it grants
to contemplative experience.

It is perhaps beside the point to notice that Radhakrishnan's
urbanity falters when he considers Christianity. As Joachim
Wach remarked: "There is a notable trace of bitterness in a great
number of references to Christianity in Radhakrishnan's
writings".[40] Such bitterness may be dismissed as purely personal
and incidental to his thesis. But it is in place to observe that,
while extolling tolerance and comprehensiveness, Radhakrishnan
openly maintains the supremacy of Hinduism and indeed of that
particular form of Hindu thought represented by Advaita Vedanta.
To quote Joachim Wach again:

It is actually a double option which determines Professor

Radhakrishnan's explicit and implicit evaluation of religion: his preference for the apprehension of ultimate reality as proclaimed by the seers and sages of India and, within this tradition, his preference for the teachings of the Upanishads in the peculiar interpretation of the Advaita school.[41]

But Radhakrishnan himself does not hide his conviction. As he says with great simplicity: "The Vedanta is not a religion, but religion itself in its most universal and deepest significance".[42] We are, in effect, being asked to surrender to a particular Hindu view of religion under the cloak of an anti-dogmatic comprehensiveness. I am afraid that the problem of the plurality and conflict of religions is not solved so easily. The religions of prophetic monotheism resist reduction to contemplative experience of the Absolute.

The mystical view of religion with its conviction of the essential unity of all religions undoubtedly has much support in the West. But this fact can lead to a hasty and, I think, mistaken identification between Hindu relativism and Western relativism. Hindu relativism has religious roots and is a religious relativism; Western relativism has a different origin and bearing. In his *World Religions and World Community* Dr Slater remarks:

> Generally speaking, our Western relativism is cold, as cold as the science which sponsors it. It is dispassionate. But the mood of Hindu relativism is different. The breath of it is hot and scorching. It is passionately religious. It is affirmative rather than negative.[43]

Later on in speaking of the Hindu custom expressed in the term *ishta-devata* (the chosen deity, the deity which is the immediate object of a man's devotion), he notes how some interpret this as meaning, not that each Hindu decides for himself which of the gods to worship, but that God has chosen this particular way to make himself known to this particular worshipper. Hindu tolerance of various ways is due to respect for the vision that may happen on that way and concern that this vision should not be lost.

> ... the very reason why Hindus are hesitant about closing any road or marking it forbidden is the fear lest the vision whereby man lives might be lost. And looking out on the wider world today, and not least on our Western world, there are Hindus who believe there is indeed ground for this fear.[44]

Within the context of the general understanding of the nature of religious truth I have already analysed, Hindu relativism, then, consists of three interrelated religious convictions. The first is that the One manifests itself to men in different ways. The Rg Veda says, "the real is One, the learned call it by various names";[45] the Upanishads continually repeat this theme.

Second, the One is in the last analysis inexpressible, so that in the end we have to fall back upon the negative statement *neti, neti* —not this, not that. Third, since religion reflects man as well as the divine, and men are at different stages of religious development, there are bound to be many different apprehensions of the divine and different ways of religious life, each having its value for men at a particular level. These three convictions make up Hindu relativism. As is obvious they constitute a positive attitude to religion, not religious indifference. Indeed, they are powerful elements that cannot be ignored in any account of religious faith.

The relativism dominant in the West is of a different quality. It marks a fading of religious faith under the impact of empiricism and rationalism.

An unfortunate consequence of the Christian stress upon mythological revelation, or the revelation of God through earthly events and their prophetic interpretation, has been an excessive concern with the intellectual element in religious faith and with creedal formulations. Faith has been reduced almost without remainder to belief, understood as the acceptance of a set of religious doctrines. When thus isolated from the other elements in religious faith, belief becomes merely a weak form of intellectual assent, one made on inadequate evidence and beset with uncertainty. Such belief sank lower in prestige as the scientific method became an ideal in the West and empirically verified knowledge the intellectual norm. The rationalist attempt to ground religious belief upon irrefragable demonstration survived neither the scepticism of Hume nor the criticism of Kant, and its failure simply deepened the sense that religious belief was an assent on inadequate evidence, though perhaps a morally and socially valuable one. For many today religious belief falls into the class of personal preferences, where a tenuous assent may be given to a particular opinion for a variety of reasons, but where it is out of place to challenge another's opinion in the name of truth. Here is a religious relativism that is empty because devoid of the core of a positive religious faith. The question we must later confront is whether we can reformulate the relation between doctrinal belief and religious faith without losing the Christian stress upon mythological revelation.

The contrast between Hindu and Western relativism does not mean that Hindu relativism is immune from the danger of deteriorating into the irreligious relativism of the West under the pressure of secularism. The cheerful acceptance of contradictions in religion is harder for men with a modern secular education. As Philip Ashby points out in *The Conflict of Religions*: "No longer can Hinduism smile benevolently upon conflicting theological beliefs as it once did. Modern man, be he Eastern or Western, demands integrity and consistency of thought to a degree unknown in India in the past".[46] To avoid a slide into secular relativism, the religious contradictions, if not eliminated, will have to be expressly harmonised as partial and fragmentary views of ultimate reality. But this implies a claim to know the truth to which all these partial views point and in relation to which they are fragmentary. The modern Hindu claim is that ultimate reality is apprehended in mystical experience and that this provides the criterion for judging the many partial formulations of that same reality. However, apart from the fact that neither this experience nor its interpretation will go without challenge in the modern secular world, there is, as Ninian Smart maintains,[47] its failure to account for the central experience of other religions, namely that of prophetic theism. This failure undermines the Hindu claim to be the true or most comprehensive religion, because such a claim implies that the claimant can make sense of other world religions and their religious experience. Since Hindu relativism has no undisputed solution to the conflict of religions, it is as open as other religions are to the secular depreciation of all religious certitude on the ground of the confused variety of religious opinion and the lack of any generally accepted criteria of religious truth.

I entered into the examination of modern Hindu comprehensiveness from a discussion of the *a priori* hostility towards the Christian claim of universality and finality for the revelation of Christ. That hostility undoubtedly exists, but what I have been arguing is that there are insufficient reasons for yielding before it. There is no self-evidently right solution to religious plurality and conflict, and one must proceed by respecting all the data, including the traditional but now unpopular conviction of a unique and final revelation in Christ.

It is time now to formulate the problem of Christ and the world religions more precisely.

This problem is one of a cluster of problems arising from the place assigned to Christ in the New Testament and subsequently in Christian tradition. Jesus Christ is presented as the one and universal Saviour. "For of all the names in the world given to men, this is the only one by which we can be saved" (Acts 4:12).[48] Again, "For there is only one God, and there is only one mediator between God and mankind, himself a man, Christ Jesus, who sacrificed himself as a ransom for them all" (I Tim. 2.5–6). There is little point in multiplying texts; the conviction that Jesus of Nazareth is the promised Saviour of all mankind runs right through the New Testament. The primitive profession of faith, "Jesus is the Lord", reaches a culmination of development in the "Great Christology" of Colossians:

He is the image of the unseen God
and the first-born of all creation,
for in him were created
all things in heaven and on earth:
everything visible and everything invisible,
Thrones, Dominations, Sovereignties, Powers—
all things were created through him and for him.
Before anything was created, he existed,
and he holds all things in unity.
Now the Church is his body,
he is its head.

As he is the Beginning,
he was first to be born from the dead,
so that he should be first in every way;
because God wanted all perfection
to be found in him
and all things to be reconciled through him and for him,
everything in heaven and everything on earth,
when he made peace
by his death on the cross

(Col. 1:15–20).

Here we have talk of the pre-existent Christ who is the head of all creation; but the pre-existent Christ is the same as he who, as Jesus of Nazareth, died on the cross and rose again, and by his death and resurrection became the head of the new creation, the Church, and of all reconciled through him and for him.

The problems that arise from the exalted position thus given to Jesus Christ in the faith of the Church are many and various. I am not here directly concerned with those concerning the person of Jesus, but rather with various facets of the Christian exclusiveness that has resulted from this faith in Christ.

In the doctrine of the supremacy of Jesus Christ there is a tension between universalism and particularity. The higher the position granted to Christ, the more widespread must be his presence and action. The supreme exaltation outlined in Colossians implies a universal active presence throughout creation and in the whole of human history. This provides a foundation for a Logos doctrine such as it was developed by Justin and the other early Christian apologists, which attributed all the manifestations of pagan wisdom to Christ as the pre-existent Logos. Along these lines lies the possibility of a Christian universalism that in all religions would see the work of Christ. On the other hand, the exalted Christ is the same Jesus who died on the cross for our sins and rose again for our justification, and this is the Good News which is the power of God saving all who have faith. How, then, can men be saved unless they hear of the man Jesus and his saving work and have faith in his name? The historical particularity of Jesus, Lord and Christ, is the source of Christian exclusiveness.

Exclusiveness has been more prominent than universalism in Christian history. And since the outlook was, as Hans Küng remarks,[49] ecclesiocentric rather than theocentric or Christocentric, discussion revolved around the axiom *Extra Ecclesiam nulla salus* ("Outside the Church no salvation"). Linked to the principle of the necessity of the Church were the principles of the necessity of baptism and the necessity of an explicit faith in Christ, this understood as requiring belief in the doctrines of the Trinity and the Incarnation. As a naïve Christian exclusiveness, ignoring the destiny of non-Christians or assigning them to eternal damnation, began to recede in the fifteenth century when the opening up of the world by the voyages of discovery made it implausible, the problem arising from those principles called for a solution. How can the unevangelised and unchurched while remaining unevangelised and unchurched be saved? Can salvation be considered as open to unbelievers without destroying the very *raison d'être* of the Gospel?

The theological debate took place, unless my ignorance deceives me, largely within Roman Catholic theology. Orthodox Protestantism remained content much longer with a narrow exclusiveness or at least refused to speculate how God might save the unevangelised. As far as we knew or were concerned, so the attitude went, there was only one way of salvation: faith in the Gospel when preached. As for Liberal Protestantism, it rejected Christian exclusiveness too readily for it to create a theological problem.

The Roman Catholic discussions approached the matter from the standpoint of individual salvation. Even though large groups and immense numbers were involved, the question was always how the unevangelised individual could be related to Christ and his salvation, reach supernatural faith and love and be linked somehow to the Catholic Church. Other religions as social entities were either ignored or regarded as obstacles. The individual was saved in spite of pagan social environment rather than in any way because of it.

The salvation of the unevangelised was explained without surrendering the principles I have mentioned by means of various distinctions. The first of these was the ancient distinction between baptism of water and baptism of desire. Eventually this distinction was also used as a model for elaborating the concept of a membership of the Church by desire. But what underlay these distinctions and prevented them from being merely verbal was the idea of a presence of implicit faith, together with supernatural love, in the hearts of all who follow their consciences. The unevangelised, so it was argued, are not unbelievers unless they sinfully close their hearts. Grace is at work in them, bringing them to faith and love, although it remains an implicit faith in a wordless revelation.[50]

The results of these theological discussions are reflected in the most recent official declaration on the subject from the Roman Catholic hierarchy. This is in the Constitution on the Church issued by the Second Vatican Council in 1964. The second half of chapter 2, "The People of God", deals with the relation of various groups of men to this People. In the course of the exposition it is made plain that salvation is available for all men, including those who through no fault of their own do not know the Gospel of Christ or his Church.[51] The Council, of course, does not enter into the theological theorising concerning the precise manner in which salvation is offered to the unevangelised.

I have referred here to the earlier question of the individual salvation of the unevangelised in order to mark off our present problem from it. The problem now is the relation of Christ and the Christian faith and community to the other religious traditions and communities in the world. The concern is not directly with the salvation of individuals but with the function of the variety of religions when viewed from a Christian standpoint. Or, to put it in another way, it is the problem now confronting the Christian of relating Christianity positively to the other world religions.

The shift of outlook implied in the transition from the earlier to the present question is similar to the shift that has taken place in Roman Catholic thinking about other Christians. Until quite recently Christians outside the Roman Catholic Church were considered in regard to salvation merely as individuals. If invincibly ignorant of the one true Church they could be saved, but in spite of not by means of the Churches to which they belonged. Owing to the change of thought brought about by the ecumenical movement within the Roman Catholic Church, the Decree on Ecumenism of the Second Vatican Council now admits that other Christian bodies are to be regarded positively as Christian Churches or at least as ecclesiastical communities and thus granted a function in the plan of salvation. Similarly in the wider ecumenism dealing with the relations between Christians and other religious people, theological reflection has passed from the question of the salvation of individual pagans in good faith to the question of the function of religions other than Christianity in the overall scheme of salvation.

The two questions are indeed closely related. The attitude adopted by the Christian theologian to other religions will influence the manner in which he accounts for the salvation of the adherents of those religions. Thus the earlier thinking about the salvation of the unevangelised will need revision. But to some extent the earlier question about individual salvation will be taken

as solved prior to the present discussion. I mean that I shall
assume that salvation as understood by Christians is made available to all men and that the gifts of grace associated with it are not
confined either in themselves or their effects to Christians. Mankind as a whole, not just the Christian Church, is under the
presence and action of God's saving grace. In other words, I shall
regard Christian exclusiveness in its rigid form, which limited
salvation to Christians, as finally discarded. This would be dis-
puted by some Christian groups, chiefly fundamentalist, but not,
I think, by any theologians of the major traditions, whether
Protestant or Catholic.

The present question about the relation between faith in
Christ and the other religious options found amongst men runs
much deeper than the previous question about individual salvation. For the latter question there was no need to step outside the
Christian framework of ideas. With the problem now before us
the Christian religious scheme as a whole is inevitably confronted
with other religious schemes built upon different principles.
Hence such points as the Christian concept of salvation, the
universal scope of Christ's work, the Christian interpretation of
religious experience, the nature of religious truth and language
are involved in the discussion and have to be reconsidered in the
light of a knowledge and sympathetic understanding of other
religions.

Unlike the earlier question, the problem of Christ and the
world religions has been discussed chiefly within Protestant
theology. Liberal Protestantism led the way by including other
religions with Christianity in an overall account of the religious
history and experience of mankind. Christian revelation and faith
were brought under the more general category of religion. There
were always those Protestants who, with some reason, feared in
that approach a loss of Christian substance, but liberal theology
succeeded in dominating the scene from Friedrich Schleier-
macher (1768–1834) to Ernest Troeltsch (1865–1923). Its reign
came to an end after the First World War with the rise of Neo-
Orthodoxy, led by Karl Barth (1886–1969) and Emil Brunner

(1889–1966), both of whom, though in differing ways, rejected the positive assessment of other religions advocated by liberal theologians.

Although there are subtleties—some would say inconsistencies—in his view and consequent difficulties of interpretation, the assessment Karl Barth makes of all religions in the light of Christian faith and revelation would seem entirely negative.[52] From the standpoint of biblical revelation, religion and religions are unbelief; they are condemned as manifestations of man's sinful rebellion against God. Christianity itself as a religion comes under the same condemnation. "Religion", writes Barth, "is never true in itself and as such. The revelation of God denies that any religion is true, i.e., that it is in truth the knowledge and worship of God and the reconciliation of man with God."[53] Again:

> . . . in short our Christianity, to the extent that it is *our* Christianity, the human work which we undertake and adjust to all kinds of near and remote aims and which as such is seen to be on the same level as the human work in other religions. This judgement means that all this Christianity of ours, and all the details of it, are not as such what they ought to be and pretend to be, a work of faith, and therefore of obedience to the divine revelation. What we have here is in its own way—a different way from that of other religions, but no less seriously—unbelief, i.e., opposition to the divine revelation, and therefore active idolatry and self-righteousness.[54]

Nevertheless, the Christian Church is the place of true religion in as much as it is "the place where, confronted with the revelation and grace of God, by grace men live by grace".[55] So,

> That there is a true religion is an event in the act of the grace of God in Jesus Christ. To be more precise, it is an event in the outpouring of the Holy Spirit. To be even more precise, it is an event in the existence of the Church and the children of

God. The existence of the Church of God and the children of God means that true religion exists even in the world of human religion.[56]

Emil Brunner's difference with Barth concerning the appropriate attitude towards other religions is part of the more general disagreement that sharply divided the two men over the possibility of a knowledge of God outside the biblical revelation. Brunner affirms that possibility and his attitude towards other religions is therefore dialectical as including an affirmation as well as a negation. Affirmatively the Christian acknowledges that these religions are to some extent a response to the revelation of God in creation and in the consciences of men; negatively he sees them in the light of Christ as a sinful and distorted response.[57]

The neo-orthodox interpretation of the nature of other religions was given outstanding expression in the influential book of Hendrik Kraemer, *The Christian Message in a Non-Christian World*. This was written for the Tambaram Conference, the meeting of the International Missionary Council at Tambaram near Madras in 1938. In some measure it was conceived as a response to the Report of a North American Commission of Laymen on the Christian missions, published in 1932 under the title *Re-Thinking Missions* and edited by William Hocking,[58] a document which in the fashion of liberal theology criticised the ideal of missionary conquest and destruction of other religions and urged an attitude of co-operation. But Kraemer's book is too powerful and original a study to be classified as polemics. He belongs to Neo-Orthodoxy in insisting that the Christian revelation is *sui generis*, so that there is only difference and antithesis between the Gospel of Christ and all other religions. He also makes the neo-orthodox distinction between empirical Christianity (that is Christianity as an historical religion) and Christian revelation and faith. Many of his statements recall Karl Barth, but he himself has criticised Barth for being insufficiently dialectical and, if we take his exposition as a whole, it is closer to Brunner than to Barth.

Some of the great influence the book has exerted may be due

to the personality of the author. Walter Horton in his essay, "Tambaram Twenty-Five Years After" gives this testimony: "I have sat at the same table with him in conference after conference on important themes, and can testify to the fairness, sensitiveness and flexibility of his mind."[59] An historian of religions and a missionary, Kraemer spoke with some authority, but also with an intelligent and persuasive eloquence. His later writings[60] have modified some details and are more eirenic in tone, but he has not in my reading changed his main thesis. His work stands as a powerful statement of Christian exclusiveness, formulated in terms of Protestant Neo-Orthodoxy.

From the beginning many resisted Kraemer's thesis, but it shared the wide popularity of Neo-Orthodoxy. That waned quite rapidly from the 1950s. The more fluid situation of present-day theology leaves the way open for new approaches to the question of religious plurality. No new dominant theological interpretation has yet emerged.

During this phase of the discussion Roman Catholic theologians have begun to make a contribution. This is coming from a group of German-speaking theologians: Karl Rahner,[61] Joseph Ratzinger,[62] Heinz Robert Schlette,[63] Bernhard Stoeckle[64] and Hans Küng.[65] These theologians start with the recent theological theme of *Heilsgeschichte* or salvation-history and seek to give all religions a place within the history of salvation, while reserving for Christianity a distinctive and central rôle.

In an indirect fashion the Second Vatican Council was led to issue a Declaration on the Relationship of the Church to Non-Christian Religions. The original intention, coming from Pope John himself, was a statement on the relations between Christians and Jews. The opposition and discussion provoked by the draft declaration on that topic led to its being treated as part of a wider theme. Hence the present Declaration. The general attitude towards other religions is stated in this passage:

The Catholic Church rejects nothing which is true and holy in these religions. She looks with sincere respect upon those ways of conduct and of life, those rules and teachings which, though differing in many particulars from what she holds and sets forth, nevertheless often reflect a ray of that Truth which enlightens all men. Indeed, she proclaims and must ever proclaim Christ, "the way, the truth, and the life" (John 14:6), in whom men find the fullness of religious life, and in whom God has reconciled all things to Himself (cf. 2 Cor. 5:18–19).

The Church therefore has this exhortation for her sons: prudently and lovingly, through dialogue and collaboration with the followers of other religions, and in witness of Christian faith and life, acknowledge, preserve, and promote the spiritual and moral goods found among these men, as well as the values in their society and culture.[66]

The statement is positive but cautious, and conceptually it would not seem to be further advanced than the Anglican declaration of more than thirty years before at the Lambeth Conference of 1930, which affirmed:

We gladly acknowledge the truths contained and emphasised in the great religions; but . . . each of them is less than the Gospel of the unsearchable riches of Christ. The majesty of God in Islam, the high moral standards and profound truth in other Eastern religions, are approaches to the truth of God revealed in Christ.[67]

But a further result of the Second Vatican Council was the establishment in May 1964 of a Secretariat for Non-Christian Religions, so that the desire for knowledge of other religions and dialogue with them has found permanent institutional expression in the Roman Catholic Church.

It is not my intention here to give a detailed examination of the various attitudes adopted by Christians towards the other religions.[68] What I do want to do, however, is to classify these attitudes in a way that will illuminate the structure and scope of the problem. With this purpose in mind and following a sugges-

tion of Owen Thomas,[69] I am going to adapt the late H. Richard
Niebuhr's well-known classification of solutions to the problem
of Christ and culture into five types to the closely related problem of Christ and religions.[70] As Niebuhr himself acknowledges,
the method of division into types is inevitably historically inadequate; the historical reality is always more complex than the
division and no person or groups ever conforms completely to a
type.[71] But the value of the method lies in its highlighting of the
motifs that constantly recur in the struggle with an enduring
problem. Using therefore Niebuhr's typology, I will try to get
closer to the problem of Christ and the world religions by out-
lining five typical solutions.

The first answer given to the problem of Christ and other religions is the flat rejection of those religions as false. Christ is
against the religions. They are dismissed as the work of sinful
men; in an earlier age they were even regarded as the work of
devils. The rôle of the Christian Church is radically to replace
them, confronting men with an uncompromising either-or.

While this answer has the advantage of clearly maintaining the
truth of Christ, it comes up against two major difficulties. First,
it hardly makes sense in the light of Christian belief in God, the
Father of Jesus Christ, as Creator of the world and Lord of universal history. Though God's ways are not ours, this view implies an account of God's dealings with men so repellent to
human moral sensitivity that it demands much stronger grounds
than can be adduced for its credibility. Second, it does not
usually withstand actual knowledge of other religions and personal
friendship with their adherents. The view springs from a ghetto
mentality and requires ghetto conditions for its survival. Those
who are genuinely familiar with both the teaching and the people
of other religions know beyond denial the spiritual values in the
religions and the spiritual qualities of the people. They cannot
put the other world religions utterly apart from Christianity and
dub them unbelief and the work of sinful men.

The second typical solution to the problem lies at the other
extreme. It may be headed "The Christ of Religion", because it

4

understands Christ as representing what is to be found in all the religions of mankind. In other words, the Christian revelation is no longer regarded as irreducibly distinct, but simply as a form, perhaps the highest and most developed form, of authentic religion as universally present among men. This is the Liberal Protestant solution, which accommodates Christ and his revelation to culture with its expression in religion and maintains the relativity of all religions, including Christianity. The religious relativism comes out in various ways: each religion appropriately expresses its own culture; there is not absolute truth in religion, only truth for us; all religions are different paths to the same goal. Theoretically this type of solution generally discerns a common essence in all religions, underlying the diversity of the historical, outward forms. The common essence is variously analysed. On a practical level the approach leads to syncretism.

This second answer has the merit of making possible a positive appreciation of the religions of mankind. There is much to be said for the moral and practical value of its generous and open attitude towards men of different faiths. But the solution confronts two great obstacles. First, it is incompatible with faith in Christ as this has been traditionally understood from the New Testament onwards. Rather than being a solution to the problem of Christ and world religions, it is the elimination of the problem by a refusal of the data. However this may be interpreted, Christ is from the beginning presented as the universal and final mediator through the event of his death and resurrection. That and not any new moral or philosophical teaching is the heart of the Christian faith. It would seem more honest to say that the Christian faith is fundamentally mistaken than to present it as but an outstanding example of a common religious essence. Second, the solution is also at variance with the fact of the other world religions. The great religions are beyond pretence in conflict over the nature of the transcendent and over man and his fulfilment. They are not different paths to the same goal. Professor Zaehner writes:

It is then only too true that the basic principles of Eastern and Western, which in practice means Indian and Semitic, thought are, I will *not* say irreconcilably opposed; they are simply not starting from the same premisses. The only common ground is that the function of religion is to provide release: there is no agreement at all as to what it is that man must be released from. The great religions are talking at cross purposes.[72]

Not all would make the divergence so sharp, but there is the growing awareness today as compared with the heyday of Liberal Protestantism that the very deep differences between the religions in their concrete reality cannot be glossed over by the construction of an abstract common essence. Religious plurality in the sense of a divergence on fundamental religious matters is the problem we have to face. The criticism of the second solution is that in effect it evades the problem.

The next three types of solution try to keep a middle path between the radical rejection of man's religions on the one side and the accommodation of Christ to these religions on the other. They seek to maintain the distinction between the Christian revelation and the various religions of mankind, but at the same time to bring the two together in some kind of unity. The issue is complicated by the problem of relating the Christian revelation to Christianity itself as the product of a particular culture. The question of the relation of Christ to the different world religions overlaps but does not coincide with the question of the relation of Christianity to those religions in the form in which it has historically developed.

The three middle solutions differ in the manner in which they bring together the Christian revelation on the one hand and the religions of mankind on the other. The three modes are synthesis, dialectic and conversion.

Those who propose a synthesis between Christ's revelation and man's religions replace the either-or of the first type of solution with a both-and. In other words, they adopt a generally positive attitude towards the various religions, without, however, denying the need for some discrimination and purification. At the same time, unlike the second or liberal solution, this solution in principle refuses to accommodate Christ to the religions, but places Christ's revelation above all the religions as distinctive by a special origin from God and as the definitive standard by which they are judged. Nevertheless, while repudiating accommodation and relativism, it still presents Christ as the fulfilment of man's religious quest and consequently sees his revelation as the crown and completion of all the religions, at least in their authentically religious elements. In brief, a synthesis is affirmed as possible between the Christian revelation and the different world religions.

There is a fair body of Anglican and Protestant writing presenting Christ's revelation as the fulfilment of the religious aspirations and partial truths found in the various religions. A typical example is *The Crown of Hinduism* by J. N. Farquhar,[73] a Protestant missionary in India. But theoretically this view is perhaps most closely related to Roman Catholicism. This is because Roman Catholic thinking is still strongly marked by the medieval synthesis between the Christian faith and culture. The medieval achievement with Thomas Aquinas as its greatest theoretician, has deeply imprinted the principle of synthesis upon the Roman Catholic mind in regard to all such questions as grace and nature, faith and reason, freedom and law, Church and State, Christ and culture. So, it is not surprising that in tackling the new problem of Christ and world religions Roman Catholic thinkers should set about meeting it by proposing a wider synthesis, a more comprehensive view of the history of salvation.

Now, to look at the problems raised by the medieval synthesis is also to see the difficulty of applying the synthetic principle to the question of Christ and world religions.

The general objection to any attempted synthesis between Christ and culture is its perhaps inevitable tendency, as Richard Niebuhr puts it, "to the absolutizing of what is relative, the reduction of the infinite to a finite form, and the materialization of the dynamic".[74] In other words, the formulation of the elements of the synthesis is necessarily provisional and uncertain;

consequently, the synthesis itself is relative and transitional. But the synthetist always forgets this and gives his synthesis the absolute character that belongs to God's revelation alone, not to any formulation or cultural embodiment of it. This general objection may then be illustrated from the medieval synthesis, which absolutised and made of divine law elements relative to a particular cultural synthesis. Much of the history of Christianity since the Middle Ages is a not entirely successful struggle to free itself from its medieval embodiment. The Roman Catholic Church in particular is still heavily burdened by its medieval heritage, which distorts its understanding of the Christian faith.

As applied to the problem of Christ and world religions the objection comes to this: the achievement of a synthesis between the Christian revelation and a particular cultural form of man's religious quest produces an institutionalisation of the Christian faith such that it blocks the way to any further synthesis with other forms of man's religion.

For the freezing of the Gospel into a particular institutional form I should like to quote this passage from Richard Niebuhr's *Christ and Culture*:

> . . . it appears that the effort to synthesize leads to the institutionalization of Christ and the gospel. It may be that a synthesis is possible in which the law of Christ is not identified with the law of the church, in which his grace is not effectively confined to the ministry of the social religious institution, in which his Lordship is not equated with the rule of those who claim to be his successors. It may be that a synthetic answer is possible in which it is recognized that the social religious institution that calls itself the church is as much a part of the temporal order and as much as a human achievement as are state, school, and economic institutions. But it is hard to see how this could be; for if Christ's grace, law and reign are not institutionalized, every synthesis must again be provisional and open, subject to radical attack, to conversion and replacement

by the action of a free Lord and of men subject to his commandment rather than to the religious institution.[75]

To put this in more concrete terms. The Christian religion as it exists, whether in its Western or in its Byzantine form, is a synthesis between the Christian revelation and other elements and forces in European culture. This synthesis, however, has led to an identification between the Christian faith and a particular institutional form of it. As long as this identification persists, no union is possible between the Christian faith and other cultures with their own religious forms. For example, the Roman Catholic is obliged to hold that the hierarchical structure of episcopate and papal monarchy, which is a product of Western political history, has to be accepted in the name of Christ by all other cultures. Other examples go deeper and involve the fundamental formulations of Christian beliefs. But if the identification is denied and the Gospel distinguished from all the religious institutions of Christians, then the possibility of a synthesis is in effect denied. In which case, the relation of the Christian revelation to the other world religions is not that of a synthesis either. If the Western Christian synthesis, which Christians have endeavoured to impose upon the East, is repudiated as a synthesis, there is little point in advocating a synthesis between the Gospel and Hinduism, for example. The relation between the Christian revelation and the various manifestations and cultural forms of mankind's religious quest must be other than that of synthesis.

In brief, a general synthesis between the Christian revelation and world religions may be attempted by subordinating other religions to the Christian religion as it has historically developed in the West. If this approach is rejected as an illegitimate absolutising of what is relative and other possible cultural and religious embodiments of the Christian revelation put on the same level as the Christian religion in its present form, then this equivalently opposes the idea of a synthesis between the Christian revelation and any cultural or religious form. A synthesis put forward as but one of a number of equally valid syntheses and moreover liable to desuetude and replacement is not a synthesis in the sense defended by the advocates of the synthetic solution, who mean rather "an authoritative statement about the way things fit together in the kingdom of God".[76]

The objection I have outlined against the principle of synthesis is strongly felt by the proponents of the second of the middle solutions. For them the relation between the Christian revelation and any religious or cultural form is dialectical. This is fourth in the series of typical solutions to the problem of Christ and world religions.

The defenders of a dialectical relation between Christ and religions of mankind see a permanent and insurmountable polarity and tension between the Christian revelation and every concrete religion, including empirical Christianity, which itself is emphatically distinguished from the Christian revelation. Christ and all religion is placed in paradox. This dialectic implies the same negative judgement upon the religions of mankind as is found among the exclusivists of the first typical solution. Human religion is seen as mired in sin, corruption and unbelief. However, the theologian of dialectic acknowledges that he belongs to human religion and cannot get out of it even as a Christian. Empirical Christianity in so far as it is a human religion comes under the same judgement as the other religions. The human religious situation is that of an insoluble opposition between the corrupt religious strivings of sinful men and the saving gift of God's revelation in Christ.

There are two main objections to the dialectical type of solution.

First, granted that it provides a vivid formulation of the Christian experience of a constant struggle with sin, it does not seem to give an adequate and coherent account of God's plan of salvation in its relation to creation. Frankly, to many the negative attitude to all man's religious striving and cultural achievements does not make sense in the light of belief in God as the one, universal Lord of creation and history.

Second, the placing of all religion on the negative side of the dialectic as corrupt and Christian revelation on the other creates the tendency to envisage the Christian revelation as separable from every religious and cultural embodiment and capable of being formulated in its pure essence. Thus all religions, including empirical Christianity, are judged against the standard of what is designated as "the biblical message" or some such name. But that approach would seem to be false both philosophically and sociologically. There is no possibility of disengaging the Christian revelation and faith from all language and symbolic expression. Consequently, we can meet that revelation and faith only in a cultural embodiment. This does not exclude a translation from one culture to another, but it does exclude the extraction of a pure essence supposedly free from all cultural accretions. Unless, then, we are prepared to say that Christian revelation as it exists in the concrete is always corrupt in its every formulation and expression, we must allow that there are religious and cultural elements not on the negative side of the dialectic. Sociologically also, the opposition between the Christian revelation and every historical form of the Christian religion is untenable. If the Christian revelation is to be granted any presence or influence at all in the social life of men, then it must be seen as incarnated in the Christian religion in its various historical phases.

In giving the second objection I have spoken of a "tendency", because the paradoxical language of dialectical theologians makes interpretation difficult. Perhaps their statements should be judged as dramatic expressions of experience rather than as philosophical accounts of the objective state of affairs.

The third mode of bringing together the Christian revelation and the religions of mankind is by conversion. This gives us the third of the middle solutions and the fifth and last in the series of typical solutions.

This type of solution may be headed "Christ the Transformer of Religion". Conversionists, unlike the dialectical theologians, view human religious striving and man's religions positively. But they have a greater sense of human sin, corruption and blindness than the synthetists. Despite sin, nature and man remain good in themselves; but because of sin they reach their true end only under the redemptive action of God and the transformation and conversion this effects. We may here apply to man's religions what Niebuhr in writing of the conversionists says of culture: "The problem of culture is therefore the problem of its conversion, not of its replacement by a new creation; though the conversion is so radical that it amounts to a kind of rebirth."[77] Each religion or concrete form of man's religious activity has to be converted to Christ. This idea is expressed most forcibly in this passage of Raymond Panikkar:

Christ did not come to found a religion, and much less a new religion, but to fulfil all justice (Matt. 3.15) and to bring to its fullness every religion of the world. Christianity is sociologically speaking, certainly one religion; it is the ancient paganism, or to be more precise the complex Hebrew-Helleno-Greco-Latino-Celtico-Gothico-Modern religion *converted* to Christ more or less successfully. Christianity in India, to take one example, should not be an imported, fully-fledged and highly developed religion, but Hinduism itself *converted*—or Islam, or Buddhism, whatever it may be. It has to be added immediately that this converted Hinduism is, substantially, the same as the old one and yet something different, a new creature. The process of conversion implies a death and resurrection, but just as the risen Christ, or the baptized person is the same as previously and yet is a new being, likewise converted Hinduism is the true risen Hinduism, the same and yet renewed, transformed. In one word, the Church brings every true and authentic religion to its *fulfilment* through a process of death and resurrection, which is the true meaning of conversion: real Christianity being the *fulfilment through conversion* of every religion and the mission of the Church that of being salt, light, leaven, which gives taste, illumines and raises the whole mass without claiming to be identified with—but neither separated from—the whole cosmos. Wheat and weed must grow together (Matt. 13.29).[78]

Conversion, it should be noticed, is not just a matter of development and fulfilment, but implies a change of outlook and direction, a re-orientation and re-ordering. But this comes as a transformation of the past, not as a destruction and replacement.

Two further elements in the conversionist position serve respectively to distinguish it from the dialectical and synthetic solutions.

First, it does not reserve the redemptive transformation of man's work to an eschatological future nor restrict it to those who have heard the Gospel preached. Eternal life is present here and now, and the power of Christ to transform all things is already active in this world and throughout mankind. A universal regeneration is therefore taking place in human history, which is not just an unresolved dialectic between sinful man and the forgiveness of God, but the overcoming of the conflict in the conversion of men and the spiritual transformation of their lives.

Second, this conversion, however, though it has decisive moments, is a continuous, never-ending process. Men can never rest in their present achievement and defend it as a normative synthesis, sufficiently representing God's plan for the ordering of creation and history. The synthetic solution to the problem of Christ and culture is static and does not take account of pluriformity and change in history. Culture is regarded as single and normative, corresponding to the essential, unchanged nature of man. But in fact history is open-ended; man is a free, intelligent subject, with a power of making himself and his world; cultures are many and various; and culture in general is on the move and open to change. Corresponding to this dynamic understanding of culture is the dynamic process of conversion, in which man is constantly under the transforming action of Christ. The same principles apply in the sphere of religion. The Christian religion at any one phase of its development is still subject to conversion, with the re-orientation and re-ordering this implies. In and through a renewed conversion it can break out of its present boundaries and perhaps meet other religions involved in the same conversion, so that there comes about a common reconception and reconstruction.

The difficulty facing the conversionist solution concerns the springboard or motivation of conversion. If in line with the objection to the previous view one refuses to suppose that a pure essence of the Christian revelation can be extracted and formulated apart from any cultural embodiment, then Christ as motivating a conversion is Christ as presented in the Christian religion of a particular time and culture. But this leaves intact the problem of relating historical Christianity, which belongs to a particular culture, and religions very different in their cultural form. The basic difficulty of relating religions is not that they give different answers, but that they ask different questions. As Wilfred Cantwell Smith remarks:

> One of the facile fallacies that students of comparative religion must early learn to outgrow is, we have felt, the supposition that the different religions give differing answers to essentially the same questions. We would hold that rather their distinctiveness lies in considerable part in a tendency to ask different questions.[79]

The question is not so much whether men of other religions continue to reject Christ, but rather whether the event and message of Christ is relevant in its very meaning to forms of the human religious quest outside the Semitic and Western tradition. In brief, the conversionist retains a conviction of the universal, transcultural significance of Christ which meets with considerable difficulty in the light of the history of religions.

On the other hand, if the process of common conversion on the part of all religions, with a resultant higher unity, is envisaged as taking place without any special reference to Christ, we are back to the liberal solution and the objection that it is incompatible with faith in Christ. The difficulty confronting the conversionist solution would therefore seem to be that difficulty inseparable from faith in the finality and universality of Christ.

I have outlined five typical solutions to the problem of the relation between Christ and the different world religions. This completes my general presentation of the question. Before going on to analyse some ideas I consider relevant to further progress in this area, let me conclude this part of the present investigation by warning against a subtle form of conservatism. A reaction against past Christian arrogance can lead one to an attitude of indiscriminately defending all the ideas, customs, practices of the various religious traditions. But as Western Christians themselves are discovering again today after a period of conservative stagnation, the Christian faith is a revolutionary force in human history. It shatters the existing framework of men's ideas and causes an upheaval in their institutions and activities. At a time when the whole world is in a revolutionary ferment, Christians will not serve men of other religions nor do justice to their own faith by assuming the role of defenders of obsolete religious ideas and customs. Their policy should not be to soften the revolutionary impact of the Christian faith, but to make sure that that impact is first directed to the ossified structure of their own Christian religion.[80]

II

FAITH AND THE RELIGIONS

II

FAITH AND THE RELIGIONS

Christian scholars who are working in the history of religions have a sense that the theological problem raised for the Christian faith by religious plurality has not yet been adequately considered, let alone satisfactorily solved.

To give some examples:

E. G. Parrinder observes: "Christian appreciation of other religions has grown very much in this century, and it presents a problem that theology has hardly tackled."[1] The German scholar, Ernst Benz, writes: "One of the most important tasks of contemporary Christian scholarship would be to set forth a new theology of the history of religions."[2]

However, the most forceful statement I have found is this by Wilfred Cantwell Smith, the distinguished Director of the Center for the Study of World Religions at Harvard University:

Now my own view here is basically quite simple: namely, that the Church has as yet not produced an adequate theology in the field of relations with other men. Christian theories of comparative religion (and for that matter other theories of comparative religion, too) have not yet been satisfactorily worked out. In the Church in earlier centuries this was attempted by men who simply did not know, and certainly did not understand, the faith of the other great religious traditions of mankind. To be quite frank, they often just did not know what they were talking about. A revision of their views is therefore necessary. I affirm, with serious conviction, that a new and truer Christian theology in this matter is today needed, and is today possible—a theology that will be truer, because more truly Christian. I am also reasonably confident that it will, in fact, be forthcoming; though I admit the matter is urgent, and I could wish more theologians were tackling the problem than is actually the case.[3]

This passage not merely expresses dissatisfaction, but also indicates the reason for the unsatisfactory state of the question and for the difficulty the question presents. In brief, the question is not one that can be answered by *a priori* theological reasoning; it demands a careful consideration of the concrete data of religious history and religious experience. So far Christian theologians have worked with an insufficient knowledge and understanding of other religious traditions. But on the assumption of the universal presence of God's grace, to study the religious history of mankind is to learn how God's grace has been active and manifested among men. For that reason theologians cannot ignore the religious facts. Just as the opening up of the world in the fifteenth and sixteenth centuries altered the data of the problem concerning the salvation of the unevangelised and led to fresh theological thinking, so, too, familiarity with the data of the different religions inevitably transforms theological theorising on their relation to Christ. The theological question of Christ and world religions can be properly tackled only by the use both of theological principles and of an intimate, thorough knowledge of the various religions. But this at once reveals the difficulty of the problem: it is beyond the competence of any one man. Like most serious questions today, it demands group endeavour and the coming together of many partial contributions, each contribution being checked and corrected by the others.

Much work remains to be done before it can be said that Christian theology is taking adequate account of the data from other religions. My own competence in the history of religions is very limited, but as a theologian stimulated by the work being done in that field I want to offer a contribution to the question of Christianity and other religions by analysing some of the elements seemingly relevant to a solution. What, then, is being attempted is of a limited, though I hope of a useful, nature.

A question arising at the outset is: does it make sense to talk of relating Christianity to other religions or, for that matter, of relating any one religion to any other? Are we not in doing so being deceived by our own abstractions and thus creating a false problem?

This line of questioning is provoked by Wilfred Cantwell Smith's book, *The Meaning and End of Religion*.[4] There he argues that the word "religion" in the sense in which it is given a plural as "religions" represents a false reification. "Neither religion in general", he writes, "nor any one of the religions, I will contend, is in itself an intelligible entity, a valid object of inquiry or of concern either for the scholar or for the man of faith."[5] He urges, unnecessarily perhaps, that the word should be dropped. The only sound meaning it has makes it equivalent to "religiousness", but there are a variety of words available to convey that concept. The other, more usual meaning falsely suggests that there are real entities corresponding to the confused abstractions we call religions.

If now we ask what corresponds in reality to what we have clumsily conceived and reified as "religions", Wilfred Smith replies:

> ... what men have tended to conceive as religion and especially as a religion can more rewardingly, more truly be conceived in terms of two factors, different in kind, both dynamic: an historical "cumulative tradition", and the personal faith of men and women.[6]

First, then, there is the personal faith of people. Faith in reality is personal and historical, not an abstract, unchanging essence we can call Christian faith or Buddhist faith. It inevitably varies from person to person and within the same person from one time to another. Faith is the way a man personally responds to the universe and the transcendent. But, in the second place, the

5

manner in which the person responds to the universe and the transcendent is made available to him by a cumulative tradition, which is the result of the faith of men in the past. His own faith then actively contributes to and modifies that cumulative tradition.

Two dynamic, ever-changing factors are therefore concealed when what in reality is a complex and shifting state of affairs is designated as a religion and given a name such as Christianity or Buddhism. These factors, I repeat, are: the personal faith of many generations of people, each with his own development, each with his own approach to the religious tradition in which he lives and his own degree of assimilation of it, each his own contribution, whether for progress or decay, to the ongoing life of that tradition; and the cumulative tradition, the deposit of past faith and the means of present and future faith, a tradition which is an historical process, not a fixed body of propositions or practices. In short, there are no static entities we can with any accuracy call "religions" and give names to.

Consequently, if we ask, for example, how Christianity is related to Buddhism, we are faced with unmanageable problems of meaning in regard to the two terms.

What is the Christianity one is trying to relate? If it is understood as the personal faith of Christian people, then the question arises, Whose faith? There is an immense variety of religious attitudes among Christians. I read once that an author had distinguished six different religions within Catholic Christianity, and no doubt as many could be distinguished among other Christians. Moreover, different sets of distinctions could be composed according to different criteria. Hence Wilfred Cantwell Smith, because each of us is a person, not a type, denies that there is a generic Christian faith and writes: "There is nothing in heaven or on earth that can legitimately be called *the* Christian faith."[7] Likewise he says there is no Hindu faith, no Buddhist faith, and so on. One may rightly, I think, wish to question whether a particular form of personal faith is authentically Christian, but historically Christian faith has taken many forms. Further, the judgement of history has not been kind to those who have tried to impose their understanding of Christian faith upon all others as alone authentic.

The same comments may be made concerning Buddhism from the standpoint of personal faith. There is a great difference between what has been called "export Buddhism", a highly rational system cherished by Western intellectuals, and Buddhism as lived in the concrete in a Buddhist country such as Burma.[8] Here again we must allow for a variety of personal religious attitudes.

The matter of relating religions at the level of personal faith will become increasingly complicated as people of one religious background begin to draw upon other religious traditions. If we seriously hold that we can learn from other religions, then we must be prepared for overlapping and complex cross-relation-ships in the personal faith of Christians, Buddhists and others, even if some defining characteristics keep their faiths distinct. This means that the relation between the personal faith of people from different religious traditions changes in the concrete and cannot be treated as a static relationship. Further, it means that the meeting of religious faiths will take place, not just externally, but within each religious group, as members influenced by other faiths enter into discussion and perhaps conflict with their yet uninfluenced fellow members. The same points were made by Robert Lawson Slater, former Director of the Center for the Study of World Religions at Harvard University, in this passage:

Strictly speaking, there is no such thing as the meeting of religions, nor is there encounter of Christianity with Hinduism or Buddhism. What we have is the encounter of *people*, whether they are living agents or spokesmen for past generations addressing mankind today through the literature they have left behind them or the institutions which they have established.

Often as not too, the meeting is not between adherents of different religions. It is between Christian and Christian, or between Buddhist and Buddhist, as the case may be, with each party to the discussion influenced by what he has derived from some religious tradition other than his own. If attempt is made at more direct encounter, with some Christian spokesman for Christianity on the one side and some Buddhist spokesman for Buddhism on the other, the question may be asked, Who is able to speak for *all* Christians and who for all Buddhists?[9]

Those with experience of the Christian ecumenical movement will recognise the similarity between the problems encountered there and those of the wider religious dialogue. Working for unity among Christians themselves, they have found that relationships of personal faith do not correspond to Church boundaries and that much of the dialogue between different attitudes has to take place internally among the members of each Church. While the major religious groups are far more profoundly divided than the different Christian Churches, a not dissimilar complexity of cross-relationships will occur at the level of personal faith with increasing dialogue.

If now, still trying to relate two religions, say Christianity and Buddhism, we interpret them not as the personal faith of people but as the observable, cumulative traditions to which this faith has given rise in the course of history, we are again faced with unmanageable problems in giving precise meaning to the two terms.

Both traditions have a long history. At what point do we take them? It is not enough in principle to opt for the present stage. The development of the two traditions has not been synchronous. At a particular moment one tradition may be in a period of decadence, while the other is flourishing. The entire history of a tradition is relevant in determining its authentic meaning, its inner resources and its capacity for renewal.

But relating two immensely long histories raises questions of demarcation.

Two religious traditions may have overlapped in the past, so that they are elements in each other's development or even perhaps growths from a single stock. Though a mutual influence has sometimes been suggested between Christianity and Buddhism, that hypothesis is highly debatable. I am, however, here concerned with the general possibility. The histories of two religious traditions may intertwine. This has in fact been so with Christianity and Judaism and later with Islam in relation to both. Even more so is this the case with Taoism, Confucianism and Buddhism in China and with Shinto and Buddhism in Japan. It is a mistake to suppose that a clear distinction between two religious traditions is a plain, unalterable fact. Distinctions are more blurred in reality than they are in our books; they also come and go. In any event, it is necessary to have more precise criteria of distinction than the current rough-and-ready naming of the major religious traditions.

Further, a religious tradition in the course of its history and geographical expansion takes up many elements into itself from the cultures it meets. The Christian tradition as it developed assimilated much from Hellenism, Roman law and Germanic folk culture; Mahayana Buddhism incorporated the mythologies of the pre-existing cultures. When we set about relating Christianity and Buddhism, are we trying to relate all the contingent and more or less extraneous elements? But is any great religious or theological purpose served by trying to relate, say, Chinese and Germanic social customs? To attempt to delimit the problem by distinguishing essential from contingent elements in Christianity and Buddhism is to raise the question of criteria of discrimination. Moreover, as I have previously remarked, there is no pure essence of Christianity, free from cultural embodiment; and the same must be said of Buddhism.

Again, every religious tradition belongs historically to one or several cultures. Now, each culture is a distinctive integration of a variety of elements, and in the various cultures the cultural elements are differently distinguished and related. There are different modes and levels of differentiation. As a consequence the strictly religious element, however we wish to define that, is not distinguished and related over against other cultural elements in the same way in the various so-called religions. These religions in fact represent heterogeneous wholes in which are found, besides religion in a narrow sense, philosophy, logic, psychology, psychotherapy, hygiene, rudimentary science, history, legend and social laws and customs, existing in varying stages and modes of differentiation. How can one intelligently relate two heterogeneous wholes, each demarcated in a different fashion? Christianity, at least in the present mode of its existence in the secular West, does not embrace the same range of elements as does Buddhism. If a restriction to the properly religious elements is suggested, this raises the question how these are to be determined, and it will be found that Christians and Buddhists differ in their understanding of what constitutes religion.

This, then, is my conclusion. To talk of relating Christianity and Buddhism, or indeed of relating any two of the major religions, is at best slip-shod. It is neither a very intelligent nor a very helpful way of tackling the problem of religious pluralism. The questions at once arise: Whose Christianity? Whose Buddhism? and Which Christianity? Which Buddhism? And the attempt to answer these questions uncovers the complex differentiation and relationships at the level both of personal faith and of historical tradition. It further shows the necessity of adopting a standpoint and appropriate criteria, in order to enter intelligently into the discussion.

I have taken Wilfred Cantwell Smith's book as a springboard for my remarks. That does not mean, however, that I find his analysis entirely satisfactory. To discuss the book in detail is not to my present purpose,[10] but one point must be made because it is closely connected with my argument.

Professor Smith disengages and emphasises the element of personal faith. But is this not an individualist interpretation of religion that forgets the fundamental place of the religious community? Where in any case is the religious community in his analysis?

In his book Smith anticipates the objection and replies to it. Ineffectively however. He talks of the importance of the community, but expressly states that the community is not "ultimate or elemental", not "a prime concept".[11] I myself should regard his account of the nature and function of the community as mistaken from both a sociological and theological standpoint. Person and community are equally fundamental as mutually dependent and interacting elements in the ongoing process that constitutes human living and human history. Community enters the definition of person, and person the definition of community. The two cannot be separated without destruction in the real order and unintelligibility in the order of thought.

Personal faith is therefore faith held in community with other persons, and the community is also the bearer of the cumulative tradition. That does not exclude that each person's faith has its individuality nor the possibility of innovation and rebellion in regard to the existing state of the religious community. To say that person and community are essentially correlative is not to deny that anything originates with the individual person. Person and community are two polar principles, inseparably linked in their development and action, but neither one should be taken as destroying or absorbing the other.

If, then, we add religious community to the two elements of religion as analysed by Smith, namely personal faith and cumulative tradition, does not this help us in relating two religions, for example Christianity and Buddhism?

The answer would seem to be no, and to this extent I am still in agreement with Smith. Because since the Reformation, Christians have been earnest defenders of their sharply demarcated visible organisations or Churches, they can be deceived here. They may wrongly suppose that a religious community can be identified with a particular organisational form, which is then regarded as somehow permanent in the midst of changing history. The specious sense of stability this gives rests upon a superficial analysis of community and also runs counter to the facts of history. Every human community is constituted, not by the organisational form that embodies it more or less adequately, but by common meaning and action, namely by a common mind in the sense of a common understanding and set of convictions, a shared commitment and common activities. All this is subject to constant change, either as development or as disintegration. With the changes of mentality, commitment and common action, the boundaries of a community alter, communities overlap and the organisational forms no longer correspond to the real shape and mutual relationships of the various communities. When the organisation thus fails to correspond to the human reality of the community, it suffers tension and either itself changes or breaks up. This is what is happening at present with the Christian Churches. The present lines of unity and division among Christians at the level of common mind and action do not correspond to the denominational boundaries. When now we turn to the East, we find that religious communities there – I do not include Islam – have never known the sharply defined boundaries of the Christian West. How are we going to distinguish and relate religious communities in India? Or in China? The answer is not obvious and may vary according to the criteria used.

In brief, the reference to religious community does not make the project of relating Christianity and Buddhism or any other two religions a manageable one. We immediately have to face the questions, Which Christian community? Which Buddhist community? Moreover, if Christian communities are at present clearly demarcated from Buddhist communities, they will not necessarily remain so. There are already, for example, those who declare themselves to be both Christians and Hindus. To identify the Christian community with a particular organisational form, so that it is a social institution clearly marked off from all other religious communities and with a clearly defined membership is to hold a view of the Christian Church not now held by all Roman Catholics,[12] let alone by all Christians. But if we place religious communities back into the change, complexity and fluidity of history, we should no longer treat the problem of their relationship as though they were fixed entities and talk, for example, of Christianity and Buddhism or Christianity and Hinduism.

What, then, is the alternative? I think that at a theoretical level the problem of religious plurality is best approached by raising particular religious questions and dealing with them in a way that takes account of the existence, doctrines and practices of the different religions. As I have already said, the data that can be handled by any one man is very limited, but a general awareness of the entire religious history of mankind and its diversity should form the context of all serious religious thinking, which is in any case a group enterprise. Religious questions may be raised from a number of different standpoints and consequently with different presuppositions and methods. This is legitimate, indeed necessary, but the standpoint and its limitations should be acknowledged. The Christian theologian when doing theology is working from the standpoint of faith in Christ as mediated by the Christian tradition. I suggest that he best meets the problem of religious pluralism by opening up various theological questions so as to take explicit account of the diversity of religious convictions.

I am working here as a Christian theologian. The theme I want to examine against the background of religious plurality is that of faith.

Faith is a word with a family of meanings. It serves my present purpose to begin with a most general meaning and then pass on to some more specific meanings.

Faith in a very general sense is the fundamental concern in a person's life. It is his personal stance, his basic orientation, the context of his thinking and the underlying attitude directing his choices and his actions. What it is more precisely is a dynamic state, involving intellect, will and emotions; dynamic, because as an habitual set or condition of the person as a whole in all his faculties, it is the source from which his actions flow, the first principle of his living.

The dynamic state includes an intellectual element. In that respect it is a fundamental outlook, which determines the horizon within which all our thinking moves. However, it is not just knowledge, but includes a basic attitude of will. In that respect it is a fundamental option, which governs our particular choices, a fundamental love, from which our limited loves spring. Further, it is not a purely spiritual stance. Since we are bodily persons, a dynamic personal state demands images that grip the imagination and release the emotions, together with emotional and bodily dispositions that support and correspond to our spiritual attitude.

There is interdependence and interaction among the intellectual, voluntary, emotional and bodily elements that come together to constitute the dynamic state I have called faith. Since faith in that sense involves the whole person, but in a manner that centres his personality or concentrates it in a fundamental concern, we could speak of it as a function of his heart. To ask a person's faith is to ask where his heart lies. Indeed, if we mean by heart the inner centre of the personality and the source of personal living in all its aspects, then faith constitutes that heart.

Persons are not born fully formed. A man has to become a person in the full sense. The extent to which men do become persons, free and in possession of themselves, varies. Hence the extent to which a person's faith or fundamental concern is a truly personal stance varies. Everyone has a fundamental concern or basic orientation in as much as everyone is in a dynamic state of some kind, determining their outlook and governing their choices and actions. But with some this state is formed more or less inadvertently and without deliberation. It comes about more by drifting with others and absorbing current opinions and attitudes than by personal reflection and choice. When truly personal, the dynamic state of faith is the result of the person's own deliberation and commitment; not usually the result of a single occasion, though dramatic conversions or changes of fundamental outlook or attitude do occur, but of a gradual discipline and mode of behaviour.

People fail to be fully persons not only by allowing the underlying pattern and general direction of their lives to be largely determined by circumstances and by others, but also by not centring their lives and giving them unity. The degree to which a faith or personal stance does centre and unify a person's life varies. This side of insanity there would always seem to be some

unity, some general direction, and therefore a faith or fundamental concern, however weak. But some people have yet to
reach a personal faith that will be truly effective in centring their
lives and prevent these being scattered in an unordered medley of
particular concerns.

What I have been saying about faith corresponds roughly to
Paul Tillich's definition of faith as ultimate concern.[13] He sees
faith on the side of the subject as a state of being ultimately or
unconditionally concerned, a state which involves the whole
personality and which in some form or other is found in everyone.

Tillich's phrase "ultimate concern" is intentionally ambiguous.[14]
It indicates both the subjective side or our being ultimately concerned and at the same time the object of our ultimate concern,
namely that which is ultimate. Now, since the unconditional or
ultimate concern of the subject is thus the correlate of that which
is ultimate, Tillich's definition of faith as ultimate concern says
more about faith even as a subjective state than my more general
"fundamental concern" or "personal stance". Therefore I want
now to consider faith in the more specific sense of ultimate concern, although without any attempt to stick closely to Tillich's
own analysis.

A man may debase and trivialise his life by making sex or money
or power or revenge or some such limited and unworthy object
his fundamental concern. An object like these may be pursued
with such relentlessness and single-mindedness that it in fact
determines the basic orientation of a person, forms the context of
his thinking and becomes the principle of his choices and actions.
So, whatever degradation this may imply, a person's faith in the
general sense I have previously defined may be in sex or money
or similar objects. That is what he believes in and on what he
centres his personality.

On the other hand, I should hesitate to speak of sex, money
and the like as ultimate concerns even in a purely subjective
sense. No doubt they may determine a personal stance, but they
are not so much ultimate concerns even for the subject as means
of escape from the ultimate dimension of living. No one **pursuing**

them unconditionally can integrate his personality by them; he has to repress his higher aspirations and close off areas of human living. What results is a stunted person, incapable of self-giving or total commitment, rather than a person in possession of himself who directs his total commitment to a wrong object.

There are, however, nobler forms of idolatry, if I may speak in that fashion. Idolatry is whenever what is finite is made the object of a subjectively unlimited or unconditional concern. This happens, for example, if religious symbols, which point to the ultimate, lose their transparency and are made themselves the object of ultimate concern. This is what Tillich calls the demonisation threatening all religious institutions and symbols. Likewise, a secular ideal, such as democratic freedom or socialism, may be a symbol of what is ultimate, but can also become idolatrous if made itself into an ultimate concern. In these cases it is not entirely inappropriate to speak of ultimate concern, an ultimate concern that is distorted and misplaced. There is an approximation to the subjective state of complete self-giving or total commitment. All the same, there is even psychologically a difference between ultimate concern with the truly ultimate and a subjectively fundamental and unlimited concern with what is finite and thus not ultimate. The latter, which is idolatry, usually becomes fanatical, because fanaticism is the result of an unlimited pursuit of limited goals; and fanaticism we associate with closed minds and closed hearts. The person is stunted rather than just misdirected.

I suggest, then, that a subject's being ultimately concerned is strictly relative to what is truly ultimate. Only what is truly ultimate can effectively unlock the deeper levels of our being, can fully expand and at the same time integrate our personality, so that a complete self-giving or total and unconditional commitment becomes possible.

With these considerations in mind, I should now like to define faith in the more specific sense of religious faith as ultimate concern, interpreted as our being ultimately concerned with what is ultimate.

When religious faith is understood in that way, the appropriate question to ask about it, at least in the first place, would not seem to be that of its truth or falsity in the sense in which truth and falsity applies to statements. Religious faith like faith in general is a dynamic state involving the whole person. Admittedly, it includes an intellectual element, and a false judgement can have disastrous results for the soundness of the state as a whole by leading the person into idolatry. Nevertheless, what matters most on the intellectual side is the person's general mental outlook, the narrowness or width of the mental horizon within which he does his thinking, and this may be adequate for a genuine religious faith despite many particular errors, false interpretations and confused concepts. True judgements are in part a cause and condition of religious faith, in part are derived from it. But religious faith itself as a dynamic state is not, I think, to be assessed as though it were assent to a set of statements. This is because the ultimate with which religious faith is concerned lies beyond the limits of our ability to conceptualise and formulate statements. Concepts and statements are therefore never more than partial elements in religious faith.

A more appropriate question concerning a supposed religious faith is that of authenticity. Does the dynamic state or personal stance in question make for authentic human living or does it distort the person and result in an inauthentic perversion of human existence? Such a question is, of course, a matter of words unless there are criteria of authenticity which are grounded upon a reflective grasp of human experience. I want to examine two criteria, namely openness and self-transcendence, which I regard as sufficiently grounded in human experience as features of authentic human living. They may serve as criteria for distinguishing genuine religious faith from specious forms of religion, and at the same time their application will show that human authenticity is in reality a function of religious faith. I am not, however, directly concerned here with defending religious faith against its opponents, but simply with gaining an understanding of it which will be relevant to religious pluralism.

Authentic human living demands an openness to the whole of reality. As a spiritual stance this openness implies an unrestricted openness to truth and a correspondingly universal love.

Truth is an absolute value that claims us unconditionally. If we consciously refuse truth in a particular instance, we corrupt our hold upon truth generally, and we show that in maintaining our convictions we are not motivated by truth, but by motives extraneous to the truth, such as prejudice, fear, desire of gain, need for security. Likewise, although we may criticise questions and show them to be inappropriate or unreasonable, we cannot arbitrarily dismiss them. To do so is the obscurantism of a stunted or corrupt mind. In brief, truth, through which we are in touch with reality, is the function of an unrestricted dynamism, always raising further questions and allowing no imposed limits or extraneous interference as it heads towards complete meaningfulness and complete truth. To attempt to block that unrestricted openness to truth by setting limits and by allowing alien factors to create blind spots is to that extent to cut oneself off from reality and lapse into inauthenticity.

Genuine love is a response to reality. For that reason it must be linked to truth or else it is no more than narcissistic self-deception. Love requires that we overcome any narcissistic tendency and meet other persons and things as they are in reality, not as we imagine or wish them to be.[15] Genuine love is therefore as universal and indivisible as truth itself. This does not deny that there are varying degrees of intimacy with a consequent variation of affective response, because in reality we are more closely joined to some persons than to others. But it does mean that any love, of friend, family or neighbour, is in fact marred by wrong motives and lacking in genuineness as love, if at the same time the person is deliberately refusing to give others the love appropriate to them. Love as our response to reality implies a willing and doing in conformity with the truth as we know it. To be fully authentic as persons, our willing and doing, which means our love, must have the same openness and unrestricted dynamism as we should have towards truth.

Now religious men experience this openness to all reality, this dynamic openness to all truth and equally universal readiness to respond to that truth in love and action, as directing them towards a reality beyond the limits that confine them as men in this world. There is no doubt we are limited as men in this world. We are limited by the physical limits we come up against as bodily persons set in a material world. We experience ourselves as finite persons in our encounter with other persons, whose distinct personal existence and will limit our own. We find everything in the world around us transitory, and thus limited and lacking in complete intelligibility. Religious experience heads beyond these limits to a transcendent reality, which represents complete intelligibility and truth and final satisfaction for unlimited love.

By definition the transcendent lies beyond our knowing and loving in so far as these are achievable by us as men in this world. But the unrestricted dynamism of our spiritual being would seem to point to a transcendent and imply ultimate and complete truth and love. The limits of ourselves as men in this world mark the limits of our knowing, but not of our tending. We do push beyond these limits with our questions, and truth is such in its universality and absoluteness that our contingent limits as men cannot be taken as marking its boundary. So, in our striving after truth we tend towards the transcendent and through the implications of our unrestricted tending we anticipate its reality.

But that is not yet the religious experience proper. This is the further experience that the transcendent towards which men in their openness tend has in reality grasped the seeker. The transcendent is disclosed in religious faith, not as an object for our comprehension, but as a reality that takes hold of us in our being as persons. We are opened to the reality of the transcendent as present and one with us.

There are, then, levels of openness to reality. There is first the openness that is mere capacity, and this is prior to any personal development. Secondly, there is the openness belonging to a developed person who in integrating his personality at successive stages of growth has kept an unrestricted openness to truth and love and overcome the many obstacles that arise to block this. There is, thirdly, the openness that is a gift from the transcendent, an expansion of being that comes from the reality of the transcendent experienced as present. Religious faith is openness in this third sense, though it both presupposes and completes openness in the other two senses.

To understand better, however, what is meant by the gift and presence of the transcendent, it is helpful to turn to the second criterion of religious faith, namely self-transcendence.

Human living for its authenticity requires self-transcendence. There are various levels at which the self is transcended.[16]

First, there is the self-transcendence involved in seeking the truth through knowledge. In our knowing we aim at reaching the truth concerning things as they are. We seek to know what is or is not so in reality, independently of ourselves. The statements we make as true intend to state what would still be so even if we the subjects making the statements did not exist. Likewise, it is the hope of the scientist or scholar to make a contribution to the natural or social sciences, to philosophy, history or other discipline, which will live on after him. Such is the objectivity knowledge strives for, however difficult it may be to achieve, however partial the achievement. And in this sense all knowing is a self-transcendence. An insane person completely unable to transcend himself and his own fantasies cannot know the real world. In a similar way, to the extent that we are enclosed within ourselves and unable to transcend our own desires, prejudices and fantasies, to that extent we do not and cannot know the real state of affairs.

Human authenticity, I have already said, demands an openness to all truth. The unrestricted dynamism of the mind towards must not be blocked, and we must be prepared to face reality as it is, to look at things as they are. The forward thrust of questioning should not be fettered or restricted by personal prejudice or group bias. In brief, we must not close our minds, but be ready constantly to transcend ourselves and our convictions when led to do so by further questions.

Such openness to truth is not a purely intellectual achievement. It depends upon the other elements in the dynamic state that constitutes our personal stance. In other words, self-transcendence is not just cognitional, and cognitional self-transcendence depends upon our transcending ourselves in our willing and doing as well as in our knowing.

There is in the second place moral self-transcendence. This occurs when we deliberate concerning values, then decide and act. The question of values arises when we are considering projects, proposals, possible courses of action; in short, when we are asking what we shall do. We ask ourselves whether the project is worth while, the proposal sound, the course of action truly good. To live authentically, that is in a truly human fashion, we have to deliberate and choose in a manner that transcends the self. We may not simply follow our self-interest and identify the good with what suits ourselves and our private advantage. Further, we may not simply go along with group interests and identify the good with whatever promotes the concern of a particular group. Indeed, we should not even promote the interests of present mankind at the cost of mankind's future. In brief, values have to be weighed and chosen in a universal context, where no relevant consideration is blocked by individual or group egoism. This is what is meant by moral self-transcendence.

However, a person does not achieve self-transcendence by himself in isolation. He can do so only if he is joined in love to other persons. No one who closes himself from love will overcome an egotistic bias in his knowing and in his assessment of values. Being in love always brings about a transvaluation of values, namely a shift in the relative importance of what we desire and pursue.

Thirdly, then, being in love is itself a form of self-transcendence. It is realised in several different though related ways.

There is intimate love, found notably between husband and wife, but also realised in other forms of intimate interpersonal

6

relationship. Psychologically, such love would seem to be a necessary presupposition for other forms of being in love. People who have never known intimate interpersonal love are usually unable to attain more general forms of love. But besides, this intimate love, there is love of one's fellow-men according to wider communities. Thus, there is the love of one's companions of work and leisure, of one's fellow-countrymen, and finally for all men. In ordinary speech we do not use such phrases as "being in love" or "falling in love" for these wider forms of love, but they are instances of self-transcendence in the order of love. Moreover, if intimate love is the psychological presupposition of the wider forms of love, it is the clearly unavoidable self-transcendence demanded by the wider forms of love that protects intimate love from the distortion caused by egoism and narcissism.

Now, in the last place, beyond the widest philanthropy and humanism as the supreme form of self-transcendence, lies the religious experience of being in love with the transcendent. It may seem strange to speak of being in love with the transcendent, but this would seem to be the universal religious experience, whatever its different modes and however it may be conceptualised. The experience which religious men have and seek to deepen is that of oneness with the transcendent, the ultimate, the holy, the true reality. And because this oneness is with the transcendent, it is gift. The oneness is not a reality produced by men. It is a state of being grasped by the transcendent. An analogy, used sometimes even where the transcendent is conceived impersonally, is the subject-to-subject union of intimate love. The fundamental relation with the transcendent in religious faith is not a relation with the transcendent as object, but a real oneness of the subject as subject with the transcendent. The reality of the subject becomes one with the reality of transcendent as given and present. This involves the highest form of self-transcendence, in which the self by its reception and acceptance of the descent of the transcendent surrenders itself into its encompassing reality.

Being grasped by the transcendent is in the conscious order, because it is a gift given to subjects as conscious. Even, therefore, in its perhaps unnoticed beginnings, it will affect the content and quality of our subjective awareness. When more strongly felt, it may enrapture the subject. But subjective awareness is not the same as objective knowledge, with its reflective grasp of the matter, leading to concepts and statements and making talk possible. In that sense the oneness with the transcendent may remain unknown, and furthermore the attempts to objectify the subjective experience may lead to a variety and clash of inter-pretations. Fundamentally the state of being grasped by the transcendent is a state of love, not of knowledge. But like other forms of being in love, though more profoundly, it alters the person's mental outlook, affects his thinking and judgement and changes his values.

I think I might well at this point sum up what I have been saying about the nature of religious faith.

Religious faith is a dynamic state involving the whole person, intellectually, volitionally and affectively, emotionally. In that respect it belongs to the general category of fundamental concern or personal stance, namely the habitual set of the person, which governs the way he lives.

Among the various dynamic states of fundamental concern, religious faith is specified as ultimate concern, which means a state of being ultimately concerned with what is ultimate.

But ultimate concern is as a subjective state qualitatively different from other, even fundamental concerns. It is not just a question of directing the same kind of concern as before to what is ultimate. Religious faith or ultimate concern involves tran-sition to a new level.

An examination of two features of authentic human living, namely openness and self-transcendence, provided a context in which the distinctive religious experience was understood as an openness to the reality of the transcendent as present within us and a supreme self-transcendence in a surrender to that present and encompassing reality. Religious faith may thus be under-stood as a dynamic state of oneness with the transcendent.

The account I have given of religious faith corresponds to the understanding of God's grace in Christian theology, at least of the Catholic variety. The gift of God's grace is the descent into us of God's love: "the love of God has been poured into our hearts by the Holy Spirit which has been given us" (Rom. 5:5). God lays hold of us by his love and becomes present within us in a subject-to-subject union. This constitutes us in a new dynamic state. The state involves the whole person and affects mind, will and emotions, but it is fundamentally a state of love, namely of *agape* or charity. As a dynamic state it becomes the principle of a new manner of living. Since the state is a state of man's conscious life, it always modifies the content and quality of his consciousness, but it is not necessarily a matter of objective knowledge nor does a false objectification of it destroy its reality.

I have named this dynamic state religious faith. This seems to me the best meaning to give to the word "faith" when discussing religious pluralism. The more specialised senses of the word in Christian theology need, I think, in any event to be placed in the general context I have drawn.

The Catholic concept of faith as the intellectual element in religious experience leads outside that context to an intellectualist distortion of religion, which renders any positive understanding of religious pluralism difficult.

Protestants, however, are more likely than Catholics to object to my interpretation of faith as a state of love, because of their insistence upon the doctrine of justification by faith. Faith in that context is the trust of the sinner in God's acquittal and acceptance of himself on account of the merits of Christ. This doctrine may be well understood as a concrete mode the experience of the transcendent may take a Christian setting, that is, the transcendent is experienced as accepting the sinner, despite his sins, in merciful forgiveness. But this acceptance is a taking hold of the sinner by the transcendent and a self-surrender of the sinner, and thus the experience, I submit, is compatible with the general analysis I have given. The doctrine as a particular interpretation underlines that oneness with the transcendent is a gift, not an end-product of human effort; and further the gift of love is seen as dependent upon a prior acquittal of the sinner while still a sinner, an acquittal on account of the Saviour's merits. This interpretation becomes incompatible with my general analysis of religious faith only if the concept of justification as extrinsic is so stressed that any intrinsic, transforming oneness with God is excluded. But then, I should argue, it also becomes incompatible with the data of Christian experience and the teaching of the New Testament taken as a whole. Further, such a view of justification by faith alone makes it almost impossible to allow for the salvation of the unevangelised. Hence the persistence of a rigid exclusivism among many Protestants, the theological rejection of all religion and religious experience as unfaith, or at least the refusal to offer any theological account of how God might deal with the unevangelised.

Although my account of faith corresponds to the Christian concept of grace, I have formulated it in more general terms in order to tackle the question whether religious faith in that sense may be found among all men of whatever religious tradition. I suggest the answer that it is. I do not mean that my analysis is an adequate description of any concrete form of religion—not even of the Christian experience. The analysis is an abstract scheme, and all religion is inevitably concrete. But granted that religious faith thus schematised is found only in a variety of different concrete instances, does the analysis hit upon universal features? I think that it does. I know that here I walk on slippery ground. Two distinguished writers, Friedrich Heiler[17] and Arnold Toynbee,[18] have, it is true, recently tried to list the features common to all the major religions, and their analyses, though different in approach and formulation, do not contradict but rather confirm my own. On the other hand, historians of religion generally react to such attempts with suspicion and criticism.[19] They are afraid, with some reason, of losing the concreteness that gives religion its power and impact by a return to the Deist attempt to distil a common essence of religion, while leaving aside the rest.[20] They are also very aware of the irreconcilable clash between religions in the area of interpretation and beliefs. However, I must insist that it is no part of my purpose to dismiss the concrete elements by which religions differ as inessential or unimportant, and I hope that this will become clear from the rest of my treatment. But as a Christian theologian who holds that God's grace is universally present amongst men, I am suggesting that this presence is manifested in some universal features of religious faith when this is linked to the search for human authenticity.

There is in every religion a thrust towards and a response to the transcendent. The transcendent may be conceived as a personal God or gods, as an impersonal Absolute or Ultimate Reality or the One, as a transcendent Self or Selves, or simply as a transcendent state. These differences of interpretation modify the concrete religious experience and cannot be regarded as amounting to the same. But in each concrete mode there is a seeking of that which lies beyond the transitory world of everyday experience and is the true reality or the really real. Moreover, whatever may be the different views concerning the role of self-effort as opposed to help from outside in attaining the transcendent, for no religious person is the transcendent of man's making, so that for all the goal is a realisation of the already present transcendent, a response to the transcendent that already is. In other words, whatever the necessity of self-effort, the transcendent has to lay hold of or break in upon the seeker. Further, in every religious tradition we find the movement to transcend the self, whether expressed as overcoming the lower or empirical self and finding the true or real self or as dissipating the illusion of the self in a realisation of the truth that there is no self.

My contention is that religious faith precisely as openness to the transcendent in a movement of self-transcendence may, however variously, inadequately or indeed wrongly objectified in doctrines, be interpreted by the Christian as based in reality upon God's immanent presence by grace in men. The grace is a self-gift of God, not by way of objective knowledge, but by a subject-to-subject union. Hence as a reality it may underlie different attempts at objectification. I do not mean that everyone who externally professes and practises religion in the various traditions is necessarily open to God's grace. This is not so among Christians. I mean that the general structure of religious faith is the *locus* of God's grace and when genuine embodies and manifests it.

What would militate against my conclusion is an interpretation of Eastern religions as an experience or realisation of the timeless or immortal soul, not union with God. This interpretation is put with sharp brevity by Professor Zaehner in the Introduction and Conclusion to *The Concise Encyclopaedia of Living Faiths*, which he edited. He sees a gulf between two types of religion, namely Semitic and Indian, which he characterises as prophetic and immanentist respectively. The following passages sum up what he considers the chief religious content of the immanentist religions:

. . . the overwhelming emphasis of Indian religion is, in the final analysis if not in the immediate manifestation, on the final realization of the soul itself as immortal (15).

Granted, then, that the *experience* of immortality is the *sole* object of religion, the very need for a divine revelation is done away with (18—Author's italics).

For the non-dualist Vedānta as well as for the Theravādin Buddhists and the Jains, man, in his eternal essence, *is* the greatest spiritual presence in the universe (414—Author's italics).

Thus while a Christian would not deny the validity of the Hindu or Buddhist experience of the eternity of the human soul which they call Nirvāna, he would deny that this represents man's ultimate bliss; for as the Hindu theists themselves, who reacted against Śankara's rigid monism, realized, the soul's realization of its own timelessness and isolation is not the final purpose of human existence, which is rather that soul's union and communion with God and its re-union with a transfigured body (416).

This interpretation of Eastern religion as, apart from its

theistic movements, the experience of the timeless soul corresponds to the author's distinction of three types of mysticism,
namely nature mysticism, monistic mysticism and theistic mysticism.[21] It is the contrast made between the latter two that is
important for our present purpose. Monistic mysticism is the
experience of absolute oneness. This is the experience of the timeless, eternal self, interpreted sometimes as but an isolated individual self among other selves, sometimes as identical with the
one Absolute. It is a mysticism of the self without any knowledge
and love of God. Theistic mysticism is the mystical union of love
with God as personal. These are two distinct and mutually
opposed types of mysticism, and they mark "an unbridgeable
gulf between all those who see God as incomparably greater than
oneself, though He is, at the same time, the root and ground of
one's being, and those who maintain that soul and God are one
and the same and that all else is pure illusion".[22] Several questions arise at this point.

Is Professor Zaehner's distinction of two types of mysticism a
distinction of the mystical experience itself, so that there are in
reality two distinct experiences, one of the soul and the other of
God; or is the distinction one of interpretation, so that there is
one subjective awareness understood in two different ways?
There can be little doubt, I think, about Zaehner's own view. For
him there are two kinds of experience, one of the timeless soul,
the other of God. The passages I quoted from *The Concise Encyclopaedia of Living Faiths* state plainly enough that immanentist
religion is an experience of the eternal soul. Likewise, the contrast between the two kinds of experience is made clear when, for
example in *Mysticism Sacred and Profane*,[23] he sees the experience of the immortal soul as an earlier stage in the mystical progress, which has then to be surpassed by the experience of loving
union with God. There are indeed passages in his writings that at
first suggest the idea that the same experience may be differently
interpreted by monists and theists, but read in context they fit
into the thesis of two different experiences.

Here, however, I find myself in agreement with Ninian

Smart's criticism in *The Yogi and the Devotee*[24] of Zaehner's account of mysticism. He points out that Zaehner lumps together three different mystical doctrines under the general heading of monistic mysticism, in order to make a strong contrast between non-theistic and theistic mysticism. Are there then four different kinds of mystical experience? Ninian Smart argues that it is more plausible to think that there is in essence a single type of contemplative or mystical experience and that the varieties may be accounted for in terms of interpretation and environment.

Agreeing with Ninian Smart that there is in essence one type of contemplative experience, I should offer the following elaboration from the standpoint of Christian theology. The real basis and source of the mystical experience is the immanent presence or subject-to-subject union of God with the person. This presence is in the order of consciousness, but as a modification of the subject, not as object. As an element in subjective awareness, it may be weak and unnoticed, so that if consciousness is understood as a reflexive, introspective apprehension of the subject, it will be described as unconscious. On the other hand, it may become a strong element of subjective awareness, even to the point of rapture. This development is what is ordinarily called the mystical experience. From the outset the immanent presence of God, with the modification of subjective awareness this causes, is given in a concrete context. This context will either stimulate or prevent in varying degrees the discernment of the mystical element in the consciousness of the subject and will provide or be lacking in symbols and doctrines of varying degrees of suitability to objectify and interpret it. Hence the diversity of mystical doctrines and the difficulty that may arise, as with Islam, when the categories of the dominant religious tradition are not suitable for the expression of mystical experience.

We might well at this point ask whether God gives himself only through a wordless presence in man's subjectivity or there is an external revelation in word and event, a disclosure of God in the order of objective knowledge. Christians affirm that there is an external revelation, but this feature of Christian faith I have yet to examine. At the moment, I should like simply to point out that there are in principle two forms of theism. There is the theism which is the objectification and interpretation of the subjective, mystical experience and which defends itself as Hindu theism does as a more adequate account of religious experience than other interpretations. In the second place there is the theism which takes the form of obedience to God as objectively manifested in word and deed. This revelation is seen as harmonising with man's subjective religious experience and as leading to the deepening of this when it is internalised. But the ground for its acceptance is the authority of God's word, not the already felt conformity with subjective experience, and its truth is presented as an account of what is so in reality, however symbolically this may be stated, not simply as an objectification of subjective awareness.

This leads me to comment briefly upon the polarity Ninian Smart sees between contemplation (dhyana) and worship (bhakti), that is between mystical religion and the religion of the numinous. Now, I would not deny the validity of this distinction as one way of classifying religious experience. But it has the defect of covering over the division between the theisms of India, with their close links with polytheism on the one hand and their constant subordination to monism on the other, and the dogmatic and exclusive theism of the Semitic religions. The stress upon "mythological revelation", which Ninian Smart sees as characteristic of worship or the religion of the numinous, would seem to lead in the Semitic religions to a specifically different conception, of religious faith. At the same time, I think that the mystical element, however submerged and unnoticed, is always present in the religion of obedience and worship, whatever may be the stress upon the objectively presented word of God. To put the reason for this in terms of Catholic theology: God's external word cannot be discerned and accepted unless God also reveals himself internally within the person. The immanent presence of God by grace, which I have argued is the real basis and source of the mystical experience, is also the basis of obedience and worship, even when these are a response to the objective authority of a prophetic revelation.

To retrace my steps a little. Disagreeing with Professor Zaehner, I should maintain that, despite the inadequate and wrong interpretations put upon it, the mystical experience of the true, transcendent self is in reality an experience of God immanently present in a oneness with the person. It is the same experience which in the context of an objective knowledge of God is understood by the person as a loving union with God. But I do need to add a qualification here, which brings me into partial agreement with Professor Zaehner. There is a regressive tendency, closely linked with mysticism in the concrete, the manifestations of which can be confused with the mystical experience itself. This is the urge to escape the tension of growth and increasing differentiation by a return to the unity of the undifferentiated self. Personal development brings ever more complex differentiation and the need to pass to ever higher levels of integration. Since this involves repeated disintegration, it is often difficult and painful. Moreover, obstacles not infrequently block the way forward. Hence the desire to return to childhood, to seek refuge in a tranquil emptiness and to fall back into the primitive unity of undifferentiation rather than struggle forward to a higher integration. This regressive tendency may produce a specious counterpart of the mystical experience. The true mystical experience is a higher integration, bringing great simplicity and unity, but not destroying the person's development. Now, while it is clear from Zaehner's analyses that some regressive trends have been associated with Eastern mysticism, it would be unjust to regard all Eastern mystical experience in that way. The fruits, social, personal and philosophical of Theravada Buddhism for example, do not allow one to judge it as psychologically regressive. Nor indeed does Professor Zaehner do this. But his positive explanation of the monistic mystical experience as the experience of the immortal soul I do not find adequate theologically nor easy to accept philosophically.

The analysis of religion by H. H. Farmer in his *Revelation and*

Religion[25] calls for mention here. He distinguishes between what he calls substantival religion, which is religion as constituted by the awareness of the specifically religious objective reality, and adjectival religion, which is religion as absorbing integrally into itself elements which nevertheless have no exclusive or necessary connexion with it. Farmer defines and analyses substantival religion from a Christian standpoint, and then uses the essential elements that emerge from the analysis as a norm in the interpretation and classification of religions. The book is stimulating and valuable, but to my mind, even from a Christian standpoint it ties genuine religion too closely to objective apprehension of God. Precisely because God transcends any objective knowledge we may have of him and because faith in him is gift, it is possible to be open to the reality of his immanent presence by grace without objective knowledge of him. This presence affects our consciousness, in so far as it alters the horizon of our minds, changes our outlook and modifies the set of our affections and will. It thus places us in the dynamic state I have called religious faith, even if that state is not accompanied by a true, objective knowledge of God. However, as an analysis of religion viewed as an objective apprehension, the book is most useful.

My immediate concern here is with what he has termed adjectival religion. This consists in the inclusion in religion of elements that are not necessarily connected with religion and are therefore also found apart from it. These elements he calls subjective, because they have to do with various fundamental needs of man, which can be formulated without any reference to the objective element in religious awareness, namely God, and because these needs can be felt and satisfied without any apprehension of God and therefore apart from the religious consciousness as defined by Farmer. Nevertheless, living religion always enters into the closest relationship with these elements and takes them up integrally into itself. "In short, living religion necessarily relates itself to these elements, but they do not necessarily relate themselves to living religion."[26]

The fifth among the elements he lists is the subject's need for integration or unification. The search for personal integration and unity may be absorbed into religion and may be fulfilled religiously. On the other hand, this search and its satisfaction may be found apart from religion. Is, then, much Eastern mysticism religious at all? There we find, especially in Theravada Buddhism, the strong drive towards inner unity apart from or deliberately disengaged from any acknowledgement of a personal god. According to Farmer's analysis, it is not religious, though capable of being taken up into religion. I again question the theological adequacy of his account. For man as he is there is no fulfilment of his need for personal unity and integration outside union with God, and therefore his striving for this with genuine openness and self-transcendence is, even where he does not know it, a striving for God. And God by his grace is present universally in this striving. I have tried to show in my analysis how religious faith and true humanism coincide. Where, then, the urge towards inner unity is not regressive—and some of what Farmer describes is regressive—and where it is not blocked or distorted by self-centredness, it will take the form of religious faith in the sense analysed.

All the same, there are some who will regard as intolerably paradoxical any application of my account of religious faith to Theravada Buddhism. This branch of Buddhism does not involve any belief in God, and the gods who inhabit the celestial regions remain outside its central spiritual concern. For these Buddhists, the contemplative or mystical experience is not a loving union with God nor is it oneness with an Absolute or Ground of Being. The transcendent is not conceived as a transcendent substance. In accordance with an analysis of the world, not as a complex of things or substances, but as a complex of impermanent states, Nirvāna is conceived as a transcendent state.[27] Further, this state is designated negatively, not positively. Moreover, Theravada Buddhism rejects the ideas of faith and grace. As Winston King remarks: "The whole faith-grace viewpoint and vocabulary are foreign to its structure of ideas and values."[28] This is because its doctrine of karma and the strict cause-effect relationship this implies between the successive states in the flow of individual existence does not leave room for any unmerited help. Reliance upon such help or grace is also considered morally undesirable; as is likewise blind faith in a saviour, which is distinguished from the reasoned confidence of a Buddhist in the Buddha's word. The spirit of Theravada Buddhism is that of confidence in the ability of man to save himself by his own efforts. The doctrines of faith and grace are regarded as enervating; they weaken religious vigour and self-discipline. It is, then, reasonable to ask how I can reconcile the religious tradition of Theravada Buddhism with my presentation of the universal features of religious faith.

The first point I must make in reply is that I am deliberately giving a hetero-interpretation. The distinction between an auto-interpretation and a hetero-interpretation is methodologically important. It is stated clearly by Ninian Smart in his *Doctrine and Argument in Indian Philosophy*:

> It is vital [he writes] to distinguish between the doctrinal interpretation put upon an event, religious experience, or complex of such, etc., by a religious tradition and the interpretation which might be put upon it by some other tradition. Naturally, the Christian, if he respects the insights of Buddhism, will want to see how far a Christian construction can be put upon certain Buddhist concepts. But it is essential to be clear about what is going on; otherwise alien thoughts are liable to be foisted upon another tradition and passed off as the real meaning of that tradition. In brief, we must distinguish between auto-interpretation (how, e.g. the Buddhist interprets the data of the Buddhist tradition) and hetero-interpretation (how, e.g. a Hindu interprets the data of the Buddhist tradition).[29]

I am not therefore in any way supposing that my account presents the understanding the Theravadins themselves have of their religious experience.

Consequently, the relevant question is whether there are sufficient indications that the reality of their contemplative experience will bear my hetero-interpretation. I think that there are.

Rudolf Otto, arguing that although Nirvāna is conceptually a negation, it is felt in consciousness as in the strongest degree positive, tells of this incident:

I recall vividly a conversation I had with a Buddhist monk. He had been putting before me methodically and pertinaciously the arguments for the Buddhist 'theology of negation', the doctrine of Anatman and 'entire emptiness'. When he had made an end, I asked him, what then Nirvāna itself is; and after a long pause came at last the single answer, low and restrained: 'Bliss—unspeakable'. And the hushed restraint of that answer, the solemnity of his voice, demeanour, and gesture, made more clear what was meant than the words themselves.[30]

To the same effect there are the penetrating reflections on the Buddha's experience of enlightenment as the context for the interpretation of his negations by Professor H. D. Lewis in his contribution to *World Religions*.[31] His considerations against a totally negative interpretation of enlightenment lead to this conclusion:

firstly, that "enlightenment" stands for Buddha for some positive state of inner peace, and secondly, that the account which is given of the way this state is attained, the impression that Buddha himself underwent some overwhelming experience, similar, both in itself and in its accompaniments, to those of other great contemplatives, together with the impact he made on others, as reflected in legend as well as in devotion to him—that all these considerations seem to combine with Buddha's silence and negativism as mutually supporting strands of cumulative evidence showing that the silence was in fact the caution of one who sensed how difficult, and even dangerous, it was to characterize directly the supreme religious reality.[32]

Finally, let me return to the chapter from which I have already quoted in Winston King's *Buddhism and Christianity*. The chapter is on grace and faith in Buddhism.[33] In it the author, who has studied under Buddhists in Burma, maintains that there are some elements of both grace and faith hidden beneath the Buddhist rejection of them. He argues that even in the most anti-grace context of karma there may be discerned elements of faith and grace. Here I cannot repeat all the points he makes. But most relevant to what I myself have called religious faith is his account of Nirvāna as being grace under the aspect of transcendence. The concluding words of the chapter make his meaning plain:

. . . it [Nirvāna] is indeed transcendent of all that we know or can express. But by the same token of its utter inexpressibility it is also utterly real according to all varieties of Buddhism. *And because it is utterly real it is supremely full of grace.* Who produced it? For what purpose? Both foolish questions. It simply exists; it is. And just because it thus is, with an "existence" utterly beyond all changing individualized existence, independent of any human or other effort to create or destroy it, it can "save" man. In fact, it saves men by thus existing. It is a "gift of grace", for there *might* have been a world without Nirvāna, hence a world without the hope of salvation. *But there it is, absolute transcendence, complete reality, unutterable Grace.*[34]

I do not regard these quotations as clinching the matter. What I have put forward from a Christian theological standpoint is a hypothesis about religious faith. It requires testing, developing and correcting by those more competent in other religions than myself. The quotations I have given simply serve to show that the hypothesis is not without some plausibility in the case where its application is most difficult, namely Theravada Buddhism.

In brief, the suggestion is that God's immanent presence by grace, his real union with the subject, is the ground and source of religious faith, understood as a dynamic state of ultimate concern in which the subject is open to the transcendent in an attitude of unrestricted self-transcendence.

I have my reservations about Ninian Smart's presentation of Theravada Buddhism as approximating most closely to "pure" or unmixed mysticism, though he adds that purity in that sense may not be everything. I should prefer to regard it as a minimal form of objectification of the subjective, mystical awareness. The reasons for the restricted objectification are cultural, historical and no doubt also personal to Gautama himself, and the continuance of the restricted form is linked to the absence of worship as a central religious practice and the maintenance of certain philosophical positions. Theravada Buddhism is thus a forcible reminder that religious faith in the concrete is mediated and expressed through an historical religious tradition and in the context of a community with its practices. The mediation and expression of religious faith through a community and its tradition does not merely associate faith externally with symbols and doctrines, rites and practices, but affects the internal structure of faith itself, giving it a specific form as a conscious state.

But to discuss the more specific forms religious faith takes in the concrete is to place faith in the context of history.

III

HISTORY AND FAITH IN CHRIST

HISTORY AND FAITH IN CHRIST

Religious faith in the concrete exists only as multiform. It is diversified into a variety of outlooks and attitudes, beliefs and practices. These are formulated and preserved in the religious traditions of the different religious communities. A person comes to faith and develops his faith through the mediation of a religious group and its tradition. He internalises faith as it is found in his community, and thus makes the communal faith his own personal faith. There is, as I have already remarked, a mutual dependence and interaction between the individual and the community, so that, while being dependent upon the community, the individual actively contributes to and perhaps modifies the communal faith.

To hold that religious faith includes a divine gift does not imply any denial of the dynamics of the human situation as I have just outlined them. It does, of course, raise the question of the *locus* of the divine gift—a question dealt with only in part so far, but lying at the centre of the problem of religious diversity.

Before examining the structure of religious faith as diversified in the concrete, I want briefly to put this question in passing: Are the concrete forms of religious faith limited to those commonly designated as religious?

To explain. There is a familiar, generally understood distinction between the religious and secular or the sacred and profane. Granted that the distinction becomes problematical when subjected to analysis by theologians and philosophers. Granted, too, that religion in principle strives to embrace the whole of life in some manner or other. The fact remains that "religious" has a generally understood field of reference when used in such phrases as religious traditions, religious communities, religious symbols, religious beliefs, religious practices and so on. Likewise in regard to the present problem of religious plurality. Everyone understands it as concerning the communities and traditions commonly designated religious, such as the Christian, the Buddhist, the Hindu. But is not this to cloak or ignore a major religious transition now taking place in the West? The West, so it might be argued, is witnessing the diminishing efficacy and approaching or already arrived death of its traditional, Christian religious forms and institutions: churches, symbols, doctrines and rites. Religious faith, however, is perennial. It is now finding embodiment in new concrete forms belonging to the so-called secular realm. What is commonly designated as secular includes the emergent forms of man's religious consciousness. To restrict one's attention to the religious in its usual meaning would be, the argument continues, to discuss past religion while ignoring present and future religion.

The thesis I am suggesting is not that of a hard secularism, which denies the transcendent. What is being argued is that outside the traditionally religious and within the secular is where we now find the living forms that are bearers of ultimacy and means of transcendent experience. Some have pointed, for example, to the self-transcending concern for social justice and peace, for a new community among men, a concern which is leading, particularly among the young, to a search for new symbols and beliefs, new ritual, a new way of life, new forms of communal living. Or to take a major event of 1969: the four-day Woodstock Music and Art Fair at Bethel in New York State, which brought more than 300,000 young people together for a celebration of their outlook and way of life. Almost every commentator and observer noted the unmistakably religious character of the event and the signs it gave of a self-transcending love of others and a dedication to ideals higher than material wealth and success. Others might choose different examples. But to put the point briefly. The monopoly of organised religion upon transcendent experiences and symbols is being broken. New religious forms are coming to birth from areas once demarcated as secular. If traditional religion is declining, its function is being carried on by a confused variety of forms, scattered throughout society and often not thought of as religious.

I think there is much truth in that contention. In some respects the present time resembles those historical periods immediately preceding the rise of new religious movements. There is the same dissatisfaction with old symbols and forms, the same search for new. There is a similar chaos of confused fumbling. Whether a new vision with new symbols and forms will come from a renewed Christian Church is perhaps a question more for faith than for rational conjecture. But whatever answer is given, it seems undeniable that new forms of the sacred are at present embryonic. Nothing has as yet emerged with the power and stability to replace traditional religious forms in their functions as embodiments of man's experience of the transcendent. For that reason it would be premature to do more in the context of the present discussion than note the possibility of disconcerting future developments.

To return to religious faith in the various forms it has taken in different cultures during the course of human history.

There is a danger of seeing the variety of religions as primarily a variety of beliefs, each religious tradition being constituted by a set of doctrines. Membership of a religious community is understood as implying subscription to a confessional formula, listing a series of propositions for acceptance. Religious divisions are thus interpreted as essentially a matter of creedal differences.

This account undoubtedly corresponds to the self-understanding of most Christian groups, at least from the Reformation to the rise of Liberal Protestantism. But it is inapplicable to other religious traditions. Perhaps the most striking contrary example is Hinduism. Neither the unity of Hinduism nor its divisions are explicable in creedal terms. Furthermore, it is questionable whether giving a primary place to doctrines formulated in creeds provides an adequate model for the understanding of the religious reality of even Christian faith, despite the strong tendency of

Christians towards dogmatism. The fixation of Christians upon dogmatic belief may be regarded as a long-lived but none the less temporary distortion.

Each concrete, social form of religious faith is centred, so it seems, not upon a list of propositional beliefs, but upon a set of symbols. A complex of symbols lies at the heart of every religious tradition, and the formation of religious groups, with their unities and divisions, corresponds to similarities and differences in the principal symbols in which religious faith has been embodied.

To look briefly at the major religions from this point of view.

At the centre of Christianity is the symbol Jesus Christ. Precisely what is meant by referring to Jesus Christ as a symbol will be discussed later. As a complex symbol it will also call for analysis. Meanwhile I may note that as a generic symbol it has taken on a variety of specific forms in the course of Christian history. The glorified Christ present with us by his Spirit is, though related, not the same symbol as the human, historical figure of nineteenth-century devotion. Again, Jesus as really present in the Blessed Sacrament was the effective symbolic core of much Catholic religion until quite recently. However, each specific form has implied rather than excluded the other elements potentially present in the generic symbolic complex.

In Islam the central symbol is the Qur'ān, the Word of God as dictated to Muhammad. Others have pointed out[1] the mistake of supposing that Muhammad stands to Islam as Jesus Christ stands to Christianity, a mistake enshrined in the misnomer Mohammedanism, which is offensive to Muslims. The place occupied by Christ in the Christian religion belongs in Islam to the Qur'ān as the very Word of God. Muhammad's position is roughly parallel to that of Paul or the Apostles, and the nearest equivalent to the New Testament is not the Qur'ān, but the Hadith, the body of tradition originating with the first generation of Muslims.

Judaism is centred upon the Torah with Moses as its author. This symbolic structure would seem to date from the Deuteronomic Reform, when the Word of God became the Book of the

Torah, written by Moses and possessing his legislative authority. That at any rate is the conclusion of Eric Voegelin in his impressive account of the origin and vicissitudes of the order of existence under which Israel lived.[2] This means that between Israel and Judaism there was a shift of the symbolic centre. The reconstruction of the symbolic centre of Israelite religion in its various phases is a question for biblical scholars, which I cannot embark upon here.

Hinduism is not a unity in the same way as the other religions so far mentioned. There are in fact several sets of symbols, each symbolic complex having a central place for a group of adherents. The philosophically minded followers of Advaita Vedanta focus upon the equation Brahman Atman, which identifies the unchanging ground of the universe (Brahman) with the innermost essence or Inner Self (Atman) of man. The equation is also expressed in the famous sentence, *Tat tvam asi* ("That art thou") from the *Chandogya Upanishad*. Because of its associated imagery, its emotional impact and its movement into mystery, that abstract conception has the function and force of a symbolic centre. The Hindus, however, for whom some form of theistic devotion predominates, are divided among a variety of central symbols. Some have one or other of the two avatars of Vishnu, namely Krishna or Rama, as their principal symbol of transcendence. Others choose Shiva as their Lord. Or devotion may be centred upon one of the consorts of Shiva, representing his Shakti or active power. Thus, for example, Ramakrishna was passionately devoted to Kali, and in some groups the worship of Shakti takes on the features of a distinct religion. Again, in the villages of India the central religious symbol is often a representation of the Mother Goddess. Nevertheless, despite profound differences of symbolic structure from one religious group to another, there is a wider unity in Hinduism. There has been historically the social unity created by the caste system, which is given a religious interpretation. There is the general acknowledgement of the Vedas as sacred writings. though these do not compare with the *Bhagavad Gita* or the Epics as sources of living religion. But there is also a general context of symbols and ideas, which can be roughly demarcated by the notions: *brahman, karma* and *moksha*. These may be refined philosophically as abstract concepts, but they also function embedded in myths and symbols. Thus Yudishthira in the *Mahabharata* or Great Epics is the personification of *dharma*.

Buddhism likewise presents a complicated scene. All forms of Buddhism are united under the central symbol of the Buddha. But this generic symbol takes on such divergent specific forms that Mahayana Buddhism might well be considered a different religion, or indeed group of religions, from Theravada Buddhism. For the Theravadins Buddha means the historical Buddha, the man who became the Enlightened One, the Supreme Teacher and Example, the exemplification of Nirvāna. Hence, together with Nirvāna, the historical Buddha constitutes the symbolic centre of that form of Buddhism. In the Mahayana the historical Buddha receded into the background. A religion of worship developed, directed to heavenly Buddhas, notably Amitabha, and to various great Bodhisattvas. These Buddhas and Bodhisattvas became saviours, who prepared a Pure Land or paradise for their faithful, where conditions were more favourable for the attainment of Nirvāna. Hope of reception into the Pure Land of Amitabha took the place for some of Nirvāna as a goal. The means of salvation was now the invocation of the heavenly Buddha in faith. Thus, Mahayana Buddhism developed a new symbolic complex. Nevertheless, it did not become entirely divorced from its origins. The contemplative ideal remained prominent through the Sangha or monastic order. Philosophically a synthesis of the divergent elements was achieved in the Three-Body doctrine. There are three bodies or aspects of the Buddha. There is the transformation-body at the human level. The various heavenly Buddhas are manifestations of the Buddha in his enjoyment-body or body of spiritual bliss. At the deepest level there is the *dharmakaya*, the body of *dharma* or truth, essence, being. At that level Buddha means the impersonal, undifferentiated Absolute or Ultimate; the second or heavenly level consists of personal, differentiated forms of the Buddha-essence; the third level is the

earthly manifestation of these. In that philosophical form Mahayana Buddhism is similar in structure to Advaita Vedanta.

What I have given is merely some rough indication of the
different sets of symbols at the centre of various religious traditions. These indications were not intended as an adequate presentation, let alone a detailed analysis, of the symbolic complex of
the major religions. I simply wanted to give some illustrations of
what I meant by a central set of symbols before beginning the
theoretical discussion of the symbolic structure of religious faith.
To turn now to that discussion.

Why speak of symbols here? Or, in other words, what precisely is meant by symbol in this context?

I speak of symbols because, although reflective thought does
derive abstract concepts and theoretical propositions from the
religious matrix, the original meaning or idea at the heart of
every religious tradition is embedded, it seems to me, in a set of
dynamic images. These images may be drawn from historical
personages or situations; they may be linked to material representations; they may be as sensuously thin as a book, a word, a
phrase, an abstract figure. But they are images that focus the
sense and imagination, not propositional statements presented
to the intellect. Further, they are dynamic images, because they
are laden with affect. They carry, release and express the emotions, and they move the person to action. What, then, in the first
place I mean by symbols is dynamic images.

But by symbol I mean more than dynamic image. The use of
the word "symbol" implies that the meaning embodied in the
image reaches out into the unknown. The content of meaning in
the symbol is partly the known, partly the unknown, indeed the
unknowable.

Meaning is immanent in symbols in the way meaning is
present in a piece of literature or a work of art prior to being
drawn out and formulated by a critic. It is there in the symbol in a
relatively undifferentiated fashion. But a process of analysis is
possible, which successively grasps elements in the total meaning
and formulates these discursively in propositional sentences.

Such sentences cannot serve the same psychological function as the symbol. Hence they can never replace the symbol. They can, however, formulate its meaning in so far as this is understood and known. Words and sentences of various kinds are part of or associated with the great religious symbols from the beginning. These verbal elements help to determine the meaning of the symbols, and they provide an initial foothold for the process of analysis into doctrinal propositions.

This process of analysis has, however, its limits. Symbols, as I have said, move out into the unknown and the unknowable. Because of the spiritual dynamism that characterises his being, man is constantly straining forward into the as yet unknown, into the future, into the yet to be attained, and in his striving he casts up images, metaphors, stories, conjectures, hypotheses, plans, to anticipate the unknown, to express his aspirations, to give shape to his goals. Symbols are images that express the dynamic thrust of man towards the unknown and yet to come. But the religious experience is that man is grasped by the transcendent, that is by the reality beyond the limits of his knowing; he experiences, as it were, the pressure of holiness of the ultimate, is drawn by it, but in darkness without seeing its reality. Symbols reach out to this mysterious reality and include it within their meaning by becoming analogies. In their functioning as analogies, symbols extrapolate features of the known upon the unknown, and thus provide an anticipatory, provisional envisagement of it. Where the unknown is the transcendent, which means the unknowable or beyond the limits of human knowing, this analogical envisagement remains the only possibility. This limits the scope of doctrinal analysis.

When doctrinal reflection attempts to analyse the meaning of the religious symbols into elements, which can then be discursively formulated, it soon comes up against the area of meaning constituted by the analogically indicated unknown. This defies literal as distinct from analogical expression. There is still, however, room for doctrinal reflection, provided its limits are recognised.

First, there is the task of reducing the multiplicity of symbols to order. The beginnings of a new religious movement are usually marked by what has been called a vegetative period of symbolic creativity. An unordered mass of symbols weakens impact and confuses meaning, and so religious thinkers introduce order by bringing a few key symbols into relief. Next, the drive for coherence and order continues and leads to the unfolding of the meaning of the symbolic complex by a gradual differentiation between the knowable and unknowable elements of meaning. Further, the analogical process is refined and corrected by distinguishing the more suitable from the less suitable and misleading analogies and by insistence upon the *via negativa* as the overall corrective. Finally, propositions are formed to exclude false and inadequate interpretations and thus to preserve the total meaning of the symbols.

The process of analysis and reflection I have briefly described, which gives rise to coherent symbol systems, doctrinal propositions, creeds, and eventually to elaborate theologies, is both legitimate and necessary. It is the way in which men lay hold of the meaning contained in the central symbolic complex of a religious tradition, explore its implications and ramifications, relate it to other ideas and concerns and enable it to ground a culture and manner of life. In the process conflicting interpretations arise. However, a divergence at the interpretative or doctrinal level does not constitute a fundamental religious difference. Deep religious differences are due to different sets of central symbols, and doctrinal differences within a religion based upon a particular symbolic complex become important only when they threaten to destroy or seriously modify the central symbols.

My statement about the set of symbols at the heart of every religious tradition could be expressed by saying that at the centre of every religion is its myth. To put the point in that way acknowledges the rehabilitation of the word "myth", which no longer necessarily implies fictional, untrue or incompatible with critical intelligence. The word, however, still retains a variety of related senses, and this complicates its use.

The use of the word "myth" in the present context would, I think, add these nuances of meaning to what has already been said. First, it would make clear that the symbols in question were not to be thought of as static representations rather after the fashion of a material statue, but that they were dramatic, so that they grouped themselves in narrative form. The symbolic complex at the centre of a religion can usually be presented as a story or series of stories. Second, perhaps more than "symbol" the word "myth" stresses that religious language in its fundamental form is evocative, concrete, figurative, analogical, existential rather than plain, abstract, literal, direct and detached. Third, defined functionally, myth is a social charter, namely the symbolic complex that grounds the self-understanding of a people, society or group and in the eyes of its members legitimates its social institutions, customs, practices. Hence a religious myth is the symbolic complex that grounds the self-understanding of a religious community and legitimates its institutions. The word "myth", then, emphasises the function of the key religious symbols in establishing a community, indeed perhaps a people, a society, a culture, when based, as in the past, upon religion. Finally, because of the close association of myth and ritual, to speak of myth reminds us that the symbolic complex of a religion finds intensive expression in the rites of that religion. In the early stages of culture, myth was probably derived from ritual, which was prior. In more developed cultures myth provides the larger context in which the ritual is carried on. Ritual in its turn provides a strong conserving force, which preserves and keeps alive the form and meaning of the myth.

In the sense I have used the word, myth is not opposed to sacred history, but sacred history is a form of myth. Israel broke with the surrounding cultures in so far as it did not base its existence as a people upon a cosmic myth, that is a myth according to which the social order is seen as the analogue of the cosmic order. Instead, Israel constituted itself by recalling its own origin as a people and presenting this as a special event in history, understood as a course of events under the will of a transcendent

God. The events of history were thus experienced and conceived by Israel in their relation to the will of God as revealed in history, and for the social charter establishing and legitimating their existence as a people the Israelites appealed to the course of historical events thus understood. This form of existence under history instead of under a cosmic myth demanded the creation of what Voegelin calls[3] a paradigmatic record or narrative. This narrated the origins of Israel and the revelation there of the transcendent God as the source of order in man and society, an order represented by Israel. The paradigmatic record also narrated the subsequent course of Israel's history as the confirmation and development of the truth of its origins. In this record events are narrated according to their meaning in relation to the revealed will of God; they are seen as paradigms of God's dealings with man in this world. They are not presented according to their meaning within an intramundane context, as is the case with modern critical history. Paradigmatic or sacred history is in fact a symbolic form which can be classified with cosmic myths under the general heading of myth, because of similarities of structure and function. I do not mean that all myths are equally valid. Sacred history may be assessed differently from cosmic myths in its relation to truth. But that assessment is not achieved by trying to maintain that sacred history is entirely different in its formal structure from myth. It is more reasonably seen as a form of myth.

Every religion, then, has its myth or central complex of symbols, from which is doctrines are derived. That is the structure of religious faith when this is found in concrete, social forms. Now, to ascertain this is to be brought up against the obstinate plurality of religions. Even on the doctrinal level the major religions flatly contradict one another on important points. But as long as religion is conceived as centred upon a set of beliefs it is possible to suppose that religious differences may be overcome by discussion, mutual correction, striving for a wider perspective and so on. Symbols and myths are, however, intractable. Despite the recurrence of archetypal patterns, particular concrete symbols are transferable only to a very limited degree from one culture to another. Again, while the meaning immanent in two sets of symbols may be complementary—this is by no means always so—this does not mean that they can be combined in their function as dynamic images in the religious life of a person or group. To put it in this way: it is one thing to ask about harmonising Buddhist and Christian doctrines, it is another thing to think of combining Buddha and Christ or replacing one with the other as the symbolic centre of religious life.

True, symbols sometimes die or lose their force and are replaced. Again, a major shift or modification of the central symbols may take place within a religious tradition, as occurred with Buddhism and during some of its phases with Christianity. Traditions with different symbolic heritages may merge or profoundly influence one another. I have already indicated that complex cross-relationships may be created among the various religions. I do not, then, want to give the impression of a fixed situation with rigid divisions separating the religions. The situation is both fluid and complex. But in speaking of the obstinate plurality of religions I am saying that religious plurality is as deeply rooted and intractable as cultural plurality.

And all the religions, including Christianity, are in the concrete culturally particular at present. Whether any of the major religions has the potentiality to become the world faith of a coming world culture will be assessed differently by the adherents of the different religions. In any event any potentiality has not yet been actualised, and, if it is, major changes as yet unforeseeable will have to take place in the religion itself and in its relations to the other religions at present existing. Further, it is debatable whether it is even likely or desirable that the world will become culturally one in the sense of having a single religion with a single myth or central symbolic complex. Does a world community demand more than the amicable co-existence of the different religious faiths?

If now one asks about the origin of the different forms of religious faith, with their myths and doctrines, their rites and practices, then to give an historical account of any detail would be a vast undertaking, even granted the insurmountable limitations of our knowledge of the origins of the great religious traditions. Here, however, only a few generalities are required, in order to pursue the present theoretical enquiry.

The various forms of religious faith—myths, symbols, doctrines, rites, laws, practices, community structures—have a permanent basis in the human psyche. Modern psychology, particularly of the Jungian variety, has familiarised us with the fact that the psyche produces a flow of symbolic material according to the stages and problems of its inner development. Man's experience of the external world is also productive of imagery. The flow of images in man is, however, interfused with intelligent meaning, arising from the activity of thought and understanding, reflection and judgement, deliberation and decision. Just as the images have both an outer and an inner source, so likewise the activities productive of intelligent meaning play upon both the data of external experience and the data of subjective consciousness. Consideration of both the world and his own inner experience raises the question of the transcendent and leads man to embody his thrust towards and response to the transcendent in meaningful symbols, rites and behaviour.

I have, however, previously presented religious faith as a gift in which the reality of the transcendent grasps man in his subjective consciousness without necessarily any objective revelation. From this point of view man's symbolic envisagement of the transcendent arises chiefly from his attempts to objectify the data of his subjective consciousness as modified by the presence of the transcendent. In other words, man's thrust towards and response to the transcendent have their source not primarily in rational reflection upon the nature and origin of the world, but in the opening of man's heart to ultimate concern and self-transcendence, an opening brought about by the divine self-gift. In relation to religious faith as a union of the subject as subject with the transcendent, the many and various symbolic forms of faith are objectifications produced by the human psyche in its

8

reaction to its non-objective union with the transcendent. Convergent upon this process of objectification, which however remains primary, is the working of man's objective intelligence in grappling with the questions raised by external reality. Rational thought about the world both helps and is helped by man's attempts to objectify his subjective religious experience in symbolic forms.

So far I have spoken of the production of the various forms in which religious faith is embodied as if this production were an affair of the individual psyche on its own. Of course, it is not. It is a social process. The individual formulates his faith in dependence upon a tradition. But a tradition itself depends upon the creativity of outstanding individuals. And apart from the contribution of the great religious originators, a tradition develops and is modified by innumerable individuals as they react to diverse influences and changing historical situations. Here we meet the immense complexity of the history of religion, which has to recount not merely the thought and activity of the great religious leaders, but also the impact of other factors—social, political, cultural, economic—upon religious ideas and practices. Nevertheless, however complicated may be the social process with its intricate intertwining of innumerable relationships, public, social forms of religious faith are living only when they continue to embody the religious experience of individuals in their response to the transcendent.

Many different symbols may therefore embody a transcendent religious experience, all serving in some way or other to objectify the subjective state produced by the immanent presence of the divine reality. That, however, does not imply that all symbols are equally valid, so that any critique of them is out of place. To argue otherwise would be to suppose that symbols are empty, having no other meaning than a bare pointing to an utterly unknown reality. This is not so.

Religious symbols are, as I have said, replete with meaning. Although they reach out into the unknown, their content of meaning has much that bears upon man and world, the truth or

falsity of which lies open to discussion. There is no reason why
an effort should not be made to formulate this content in propositions, so as to examine its truth. Admittedly, the interpretation
of religious symbols can be rather elusive. Moreover, religious
matters do not of their nature lend themselves to proof or dis-
proof by knock-down arguments. There are too many subtleties
and obscurities, too much personal and social involvement, at
times too great a change of outlook and attitude demanded in
order to see a question afresh, that the lack of compelling
evidence is not surprising. But it would show ignorance of the
subject-matter and a failure to overcome mistaken expectations to
conclude that anything goes in religion and that reasoned discussion is pointless.

To take Buddhist and Christian religious symbols for example.
These imply different propositions concerning the nature of
reality, the meaning of time and history, the constitution of man,
the nature of his present predicament, to mention no others. The
pros and cons of these views can and should be discussed. There
is need to do this, in order to have an intelligent preference for
one set of views rather than the other. Further, as should be clear
from the examples I have given, religious doctrines come into
relationship with knowledge outside the strictly religious field.
Unless a man is prepared to renounce any attempt to integrate
his life intelligently, he cannot avoid coming to grips with the
intellectual problems raised by his religion.

It might be suggested that the religious value of the symbols as
symbols remains unaffected by the truth or falsity of their doctrinal implications. But this is only partly true. To examine the
matter more closely.

Symbols usually contain many elements of meaning, present in
the symbol in a largely undifferentiated fashion. It is possible,
then, to use a symbol as an embodiment of religious experience
without any explicit awareness of many of its doctrinal implications and presuppositions. Some of these may therefore be false
without this implying that the religious experience is not genuine.
Further, some of the less important elements of meaning may be

altered by reinterpretation without this destroying the central nucleus of meaning in the symbol. Thus, the Christian doctrine of original sin has substantially changed in recent years without the core meaning of the symbol of Christ as Saviour being destroyed. But the truth or falsity of the more important elements of symbolic meaning as formulated in propositions, do it seems to me seriously affect the value of the symbol as a valid and adequate vehicle of religious experience. Any falsity there has a distorting effect upon the religious experience itself and its consequences for living; and, if the falsity is recognised, it becomes a grave hindrance to the very functioning of the symbols as symbols.

To give some examples. The Buddhist symbol of Nirvāna presupposes the chain of rebirths and the operation of the law of causality known as *karma*. It is difficult—to say no more than that—to see how it could remain meaningful as a particular symbol if that account of human existence were denied. The Bible, as I have already observed, is less central to Christianity than the Qur'ān is to Islam. What has happened to the doctrines of verbal inspiration and inerrancy as held of the Bible gives some indication of the threat of modern historical criticism to the Qur'ān as symbol. The viability of the Christian symbol for many today depends upon the ability to find an acceptable interpretation of the resurrection.

Religious symbols do indeed stretch out towards the unknown where our thought and speech reach their limits and are silenced. We have no proper knowledge of the transcendent itself. We cannot understand its reality. But even here it is untrue to say that anything goes and that a critique of symbols has no place. Even to raise the question of the transcendent presupposes a preliminary, anticipatory notion of what it is we are seeking, and this at least enables us to make some judgements concerning what the transcendent is not. Reflection upon our experience produces reasons for forming preliminary notions of the transcendent through analogy and negation and for excluding various errors, such as polytheism. The possibility of this kind of imperfect, groping, anticipatory knowledge of a transcendent reality that remains essentially unknown is the basis of natural theology. Its intellectual work is no substitute at all for transcendent religious experience as embodied in symbols, but it can protect that experience and prevent the degradation of its symbols. It will, for example, exclude the idolatry caused by literalism.

I have been considering the question of truth and falsity in so far as this applies to propositions derived from religious symbols in the attempt to understand and formulate their meaning. This is one way of assessing the validity of religious symbols. But just as a symbol is much more than a congeries of propositions, so too the assessment of its validity demands more than a discussion of its propositional implications. There is its truth or validity in the sense of its adequacy to human experience as a whole. I have more in mind here than an assessment by psychological and sociological criteria, though I should not deny that such criteria, when they themselves can be sufficiently grounded, have their part in eliminating unhealthy and regressive, degrading and oppressive forms of religion. But precisely because religion is of its nature a comprehensive symbolic form for human living, there is the question whether a particular set of religious symbols measures up to the height and depth and breadth of human experience. An assessment of this cannot be reduced to a discussion of the truth of particular propositional items. If I may borrow a phrase from Paul Tillich,[4] experiential verification or verification through the very process of life is here the only possible method of testing. While to some extent the findings of this may be formulated and discussed, it is impossible to substitute argument for the process of life in reaching a conclusion.

My contention, then, is that it is both legitimate and necessary to discuss religious symbols, not only in respect of their psychological effectiveness, but also in respect of their truth or falsity. That does not imply any expectation of apodeictic arguments finally deciding religious questions and demonstrating the truth of one religion as against all the others. Religious questions do not lend themselves to compelling arguments, and a so-called religion is too complex a phenomenon for a simple assertion of its truth or falsity as a whole to make sense. Furthermore, to be convinced of the falsity of elements of meaning in a religious symbolic complex does not necessitate a denial that these symbols embody a genuine religious experience. Inadequate, defective symbols, shot through with falsity, may, though falteringly and with distortion, convey genuine experience of the transcendent. But granted all these qualifications, one must still say there is place and need in religion to raise the question of truth and falsity.

Symbolic forms and doctrinal propositions derived from them have so far been considered simply as the product of man's own imagination and intelligence, working upon the data of his inner and outer experience. True, his creativity belongs to a consciousness modified by the presence of transcendent reality, but this subjective union with the transcendent does not directly add to the objective content and forms of this knowledge. The various forms of religious faith in the concrete are therefore the result of a multiple, culturally variegated objectification of a non-objective inner transcendent experience and of similarly diverse speculation about the world.

But to leave it at that would be to give an exclusively mystical account of religious faith, which would pay no attention to the prophetic interpretation of religious experience.

According to prophetic religion, as found notably in the Judaeo-Christian tradition, God does not enter man's religious life only in a wordless subject-to-subject union. He also discloses himself in the order of objective knowledge through the prophetic word.

The standpoint of prophetic religion can be expressed by saying that God in his revelation enters into the public arena of history. Mystical experience as a divine communication or revelation, because it is non-objective, non-conceptual, wordless, is in itself suprahistorical, even though it gives rise to an historical process of objectification and influences men in their historical existence. Prophetic revelation is revelation through symbols, concepts, words and actions fully involved in history and belonging to a particular people and culture. Revelation through a prophet can in principle be dated and located; it has a time and place. Its origin, its development, its influence are fully part of the historical process.

There is a second way in which prophetic revelation is related to history. One of its major themes is the meaning of history. Prophets are typically men with a message from God about the contemporary situation and the events now taking place or about to occur. They see the events of history in their relation to the will of God. They preach the sovereignty of God over history. They interpret events as symbols manifesting God's purpose, his will to chastise, his will to save; and, as the work of men, these same events are viewed as obedience to or defection from the will of God. Hence sacred history as the central symbolism or myth in Israel as a people with a prophetic religion and the continuance of this symbolic form as the context of the Christian symbol, Jesus Christ.

The different understanding of history in the different religions, with the notorious but perhaps sometimes exaggerated contrast between the Eastern religions and the Judaeo-Christian tradition, is clearly most relevant to any assessment of the relative validity of the symbols and doctrines of each of the religions. Whether history is reality or illusion, goal-less and cyclic or purposeful and linear, is a question that demands critical discussion. But that is not my present task. I am concerned with historical or prophetic revelation in so far as it gives rise to a particular form of religious faith.

The reception of the divine communication by the prophet himself may take place in various ways. There is no one mode. The psychology of prophecy is complex and deserves more attention than it has received.[5] There is no need to suppose in the literal sense a voice from heaven; and the external, earthly events underlying such symbolic incidents as Moses and the burning bush and Isaiah in the temple are a matter for debate. But whatever the inner and outer occurrences involved, the result is that the prophet is possessed of a message, that is of insights, commands, warnings, assertions and so forth, which he is convinced is not of his own devising but from God. The Spirit of the Lord has come upon him, and he has received the Word of God.

A remarkable expression of the prophetic sense of being taken over by the Word of God is the cry wrung from Jeremiah:

> You have seduced me, Yahweh, and I have let myself be
> seduced; you have overpowered me: you were the stronger.
> I am a daily laughing-stock,
> everybody's butt.
> Each time I speak the word, I have to howl
> and proclaim: "Violence and ruin!"
> The word of Yahweh has meant for me
> insult, derision, all day long.
> I used to say, "I will not think about him,
> I will not speak in his name any more".
> Then there seemed to be a fire burning in my heart,
> imprisoned in my bones.
> The effort to restrain it wearied me,
> I could not bear it.
>
> (Jer. 20:7–9.)

But the whole prophetic tradition bears witness to the conviction that the prophet speaks, not his own word, but a word communicated to him by God.

If we accept the prophetic experience, we allow that God has through the words of the prophets disclosed himself and his will in the order of objective knowledge. God's gift of himself in religious faith is not just his presence in a wordless subjective union. He speaks within history, at least to some, through the prophets, addressing himself as personal Intelligence and Will to men as persons with intelligence and will. So, religious faith in prophetic religion is not simply the active reception of a mystical subjective union with transcendent; it includes an obedience, in assent and active performance, to God's Word as externally and publicly presented through the mediation of the prophets.

To speak of God's self-disclosure or revelation through the

prophets is, however, ambiguous. In one sense God does not reveal himself. He remains the hidden God. Prophetic religion by its own admission has no direct objective knowledge of God. Hence prophetic religion remains similar to mystical religion in the forms taken by its objective content. The concrete, social forms of its faith are primarily symbols, which in their reference to the transcendent are analogies. In brief, prophetic religion is like mystical religion centred upon a symbolic complex, with doctrinal propositions having a secondary and derivative function. The difference, however, is that the processes of symbolisation with the objective meaning these create are seen in prophetic religion as taking place under the movement of God and therefore as having the stamp of divine authority.

To attribute the objective content of religion to God and endow it with his authority is to give great prominence to what may be called a realist interpretation of religious language. I have already argued against an interpretation of religious symbols that would deprive them of objective meaning and render futile a discussion of them in terms of truth and falsity. Religious symbols are not just vehicles of subjective experience in the sense that their only meaning is their function of giving vent to the religious feelings of those who use them. They have a content of meaning concerning the world, man and the transcendent. This reference to an order of reality, relevant indeed to subjective religious experience but itself independently real, is much stronger in prophetic religion, because the prophetic word is less closely tied to subjective experience than the symbols of mystical religion. The Word of God, publicly presented through the prophets, stands as true whether it happens to correspond to the inner religious state of its hearers or not. Indeed, its frequent purpose is to bring about the upheaval in personal consciousness known as conversion.

The realist implications of the prophetic word are the basis for the dogmatic development that has taken place in Christianity. While justified within limits, this development has led to a one-sided stress upon the role of doctrinal beliefs in religious faith.

Religious faith as a personal commitment is essentially mediated through a symbolic complex, not a set of propositions. The analysis of the symbolic complex into propositions is both legitimate and necessary, but at the same time secondary and often debatable. Further, the recognition of the prophetic word as God's word is not achieved by proof and argument, but by the inner enlightenment due to God's presence in the subject, when God thus present wills that recognition. The stress on the objective truth of dogmas has led to an overshadowing of the mystical, subjective element in all genuine religious faith.

All the same, the objection to the modern Hindu thesis of the unity of all religions is that it does not account for religious faith as experienced and lived in the prophetic tradition. With its exclusively mystical interpretation of religion, the Hindu thesis in effect demands the elimination of prophetic religion. Prophetic religion when it retains its distinctive characteristics makes inevitable a differentiation of religious traditions in terms of truth and falsity and in relation to divine authority.

This differentiation does not deny the universal possibility of a genuine religious faith in the sense of an openness to the immanent presence of the transcendent. As I hope my previous analysis has shown, this can exist without prophetic revelation and with objective symbolisations of varying degrees of merit and truth. Nor does the necessity of a differential evaluation of religious traditions imply, so it seems to me, that genuine prophetic revelation is confined to a single tradition. In other words, I see no reason why Christians should not recognise the existence of genuine prophets outside the Judaeo-Christian tradition. Zarathustra and Muhammad are obvious candidates. Further, there is reason on occasion to wonder about the possible intervention of prophetic revelation even in the context of predominantly mystical religion. Does perhaps the theophany of Krishna granted to Arjuna in the eleventh chapter of the *Bhagavad-Gita* reflect a prophetic vision? At other points, too, which mark an advance in religious conception, one might conjecture a divine intervention similar to that claimed by prophetic religion.

I see no reason, then, why a religious tradition based upon prophetic revelation should in principle exclude the occurrence of prophetic revelation in other traditions. What, however, is required is that all acknowledged instances of prophetic revelation should be mutually compatible and capable of being brought into some relationship. God's Word cannot contradict itself or promote completely unrelated ends. Here we confront the contradictions that do divide the religious traditions. This conflict cannot be eluded, unless one is prepared to empty religious symbols of their meaning. However, it is unnecessarily exacerbated by a mistaken preoccupation with inerrancy or infallibility. There is nothing in the concept of prophetic revelation that necessitates absolute accuracy in its reception and transmission. Many Christians today have come to the conviction that God's purpose in making a revelation requires no more in regard to errors of reception and transmission than the counteracting and eventual overcoming of them through his providential ordering of history. There is no call to suppose that he prevents the very occurrence of error by guaranteeing the inerrancy of a record of revelation or granting infallibility to some agency for legally authenticated interpretations. Elements of a genuine prophetic revelation may exist partially distorted by mistaken or corrupt formulations or overlaid by false interpretations. This opens the possibility of a discussion between religious traditions not blocked by the presupposition by either party of the total truth of his particular tradition. There is room for mutual learning and mutual correction.

However, against the background of religious faith as mediated by prophetic revelation, we meet the exceptional position granted to Jesus Christ by Christians. I think it is necessary to stress that the only appropriate context for considering the place of Christ is the prophetic type of religion, as I have outlined it. If religious faith is interpreted in a purely mystical fashion and no account taken of the experience of prophetic revelation, then Christian talk about the finality of Christ will seem meaningless or the sign of an absurd cultural exclusivism. It is in the framework of

belief in the occurrence of prophetic revelation in God's providential ordering of history that it makes sense to speak of Christ
as the supreme moment in the revelatory process. As we read in
Hebrews: "At various times in the past and in various different
ways, God spoke to our ancestors through the prophets; but in
our own time, the last days, he has spoken to us through his Son"
(Heb. 1:1–2). I say the place given to Christ makes sense within
the framework of prophetic revelation. Whether one accepts the
Christian claim or not is, of course, a different matter.

It is impossible here even to sketch a Christology. But I am not
trying to give a substantive account of faith in Christ. My aim is to
outline a formal structure of religious faith, including the faith
of Christians, which allows for religious plurality. From that
standpoint it seems possible to present Jesus Christ as the symbolic centre for Christian faith under four headings: person,
event, presence, word.

To begin with a preliminary remark about Jesus Christ as
symbol. In speaking of Jesus Christ as a symbol I mean first that
he is at the centre of Christian faith as a dynamic image, focusing
the imagination, releasing the emotions and moving to action.
In the second place I mean that he is the embodiment of meaning, expressing both the objective content of God's supreme
revelation and the subjective union of man with God. In brief, he
fulfils those functions I have described as belonging to the central
symbolic complex of every religion. Now, in view of the claims
made for Christ, we should expect him to fulfil those functions
in a distinctive manner. It is this distinctive manner I shall
attempt to delineate under the four heads I have mentioned.

Jesus Christ is a person. He is not a fictional figure, but a real
person who lived in history. Although we do not have enough
information to write a biography of him, his reality as a person in
history is to some extent accessible in the impact he made upon
his disciples and through the memories they transmitted of his
life and teaching. The written Gospels are difficult material if
one's aim is to reconstruct the biographical details. Their chief
value, however, lies in conveying the religious meaning appre-

hended as embodied in Jesus by the first Christians. It was this meaning, newly present in history, which gave rise to the Christian Church.

The central symbol for Christian faith is thus a real person. It should at once be evident that such a symbol cannot be adequately resolved into a set of doctrines. Richard Niebuhr remarks on "the impossibility of stating adequately by means of concepts and propositions a principle which presents itself in the form of a person".[6] I have previously argued that in general the central symbolic complex of a religion cannot be replaced by a set of propositional beliefs. When the central symbol is a person, the point should be so evident as to need no discussion.

Further, Jesus differed from the prophets before him in the manner in which his message merged into identity with his person. This has been widely noted and documented by New Testament commentators. It is true that Jesus preached the Kingdom of God, not himself. Some modern scholars deny that Jesus made any explicit Christological claims. Christology began as the response of the first Christians to the history of Jesus. In other words, it was in the post-Easter Church that, in Bultmann's phrase, the Proclaimer became the Proclaimed. Nevertheless, even for these scholars, there is a Christology implicit in Jesus' own teaching. As Reginald H. Fuller puts it, Jesus understood his mission in terms of eschatological prophecy. As eschatological prophet he was not merely announcing the future coming of salvation and judgement, but actually initiating it in his words and deeds. His proclamation and activity confronted men with the presence and saving act of God breaking into history. What the post-Easter Church did was to interpret this in terms of an explicit Christology.[7] Certainly, after Easter the Christian message or *kerygma* coincides with the meaning embodied in Jesus as a person.

Second, Jesus Christ is an event. What took place in the life and death of Jesus of Nazareth, together with the occurrences after his death which brought the disciples to belief in his resurrection, formed a complex historical event, which was placed by the early Church in the context of Israel's paradigmatic or sacred history. Just as the exodus from Egypt was seen as the manifestation of the saving power of God and the embodiment of his active presence with his people, so, too, the event of Jesus Christ. But Christians saw the event of Jesus Christ as the culmination of sacred history. For that reason they gave this event both a universal and a final import. The event of Jesus Christ is the final, irrevocable reconciliation of mankind with God. Not by any intrinsic necessity but by God's free choice, the salvation of mankind depends upon the event of Jesus Christ. That salvation is now assured, though the working out of its consequences has yet to be completed. Since the atonement is an objective event, to experience its effects does not necessitate a knowledge of it.

Third, Jesus Christ is a presence. As a focus for Christian faith Jesus Christ is not a person of past history now present to us only in memory. He is a living person, united to us in an interpersonal union of knowledge and love, actively present with us to enlighten and help us in a spiritual fashion and, as the object of our devotion, the means of our access in prayer and worship to God. The active presence of Jesus Christ as a living person to all future generations is, among other elements, the meaning of his resurrection. Further, it raises the question about his relation to God. The theme of the Old Testament is active presence of God with his people. This becomes in the New Testament the active presence of God with his people through the presence of Christ. In other words, the presence of Christ is the presence of God with men. This implies a unique relationship between Christ and God. Christology is an attempt to formulate this.

Finally, Jesus Christ is word, that is the Word of God. As I have said, faith in Christ must be placed in the setting of the more general conviction that God has communicated with men in the course of history and in the order of objective knowledge. The designation of Jesus as the very Word of God implies the conviction that in him is embodied an unsurpassable fullness of divine communication. This does not make good sense, or at least it is difficult to sustain, if it is interpreted directly of teaching—of doctrinal concepts and propositions. Since the time of Christ, men have continued to learn religiously, and I do not see why one should try to maintain that everything they have learnt is not only compatible with the words and deeds of Christ but also derived from them. Nor have I found any cogent reason for holding that prophetic revelation has come to an end or at least can now communicate nothing not logically implied in the teaching of the New Testament. No, that the fulness of truth is present in Jesus as the Word of God is not a statement about his teaching nor about the New Testament doctrine concerning him; it is a statement about his reality. The man Jesus was the active presence of God, God's Word, the expression in a man amongst men of the reality of God in his power and will to serve, in his love of men, in his holiness, righteousness and truth. Such a communication cannot be surpassed; in itself it contains all. For that reason it marks the centre of human history and a point of reference for all prior and subsequent experiences and events. But what men receive of that fulness is limited by their restricted capacity and by the laws of historical development. So, the course of religious history continues, with its advances and its regressions and with men divided among many religions.

My analysis of the meaning of Jesus Christ as the central symbol of the Christian religion makes plain that faith in Christ implies granting him a universal and final role in regard to human existence and human history. There is indeed a variety of interpretations of Christ among Christians. But the points I have made are quite central and general. Frankly, I do not myself see how the universality and finality of Christ can be denied without emptying the Christian tradition of meaning.

However, against the background of all that I have said about religious faith, I should like briefly to indicate what, in my opinion, this faith in Christ does not imply.

First, it does not imply any denial of genuine religious faith, meaningful religious symbols and indeed prophetic revelation outside the Christian tradition. While there are grounds in theological principle as well as in historical fact for asserting the universal incidence of genuine religious faith and meaningful symbols, there is no theological reason to maintain the universality of prophetic revelation. Its extent, therefore, is a matter for discussion in the light of the historical data.

Second, it does not imply that Christians have nothing to learn religiously from other traditions. Dialogue with people of other faiths may be mutually helpful in the formation of new religious conceptions and practices. This has already happened in the past, though it is sometimes admitted with reluctance. To give one example: the development of Christian mysticism owes much to non-Christian influences.

Third, it does not imply that other religions no longer have a function in God's providential ordering of history, so that religious pluralism should be judged by Christians in a purely negative manner. This point needs some explanation.

The contention is sometimes heard that because Christ is universal Saviour and God's final revelation other religions are in principle abolished and religious plurality is against God's will. But this contention seems to me to involve several questionable assumptions.

It presupposes that the work of Christ for the coming of God's Kingdom is being carried on in an exclusive fashion by the Christian Church, namely the community of those who explicitly acknowledge him. However, to make this exclusive claim for the Church is to go against the universality claimed for Christ. If Christ is truly universal Saviour, then religions other than Christianity, which are in fact still the vehicles for the religious faith of most men, must have a positive place in the divine scheme of salvation through Christ.[8]

The contention that other religions are now abolished further assumes that it would be better for the Christian Church and for the cause of faith in Christ, were religious diversity to come to an end by all men becoming Christians. This seems to take a very unrealistic view of man and to ignore the lessons of history. As men are in the present historical order, a pluralistic situation seems best to preserve and promote truth and to ward off corruption. In view of the imperfect grasp of Christian truth and values by Christians, a Christian monopoly in the foreseeable future would, I think, be disastrous. I suggest that we might assume that God in his providence takes account of the needs and complexities of human historical development rather than insists upon an abstract ideal of religious unity.

Which brings me to the next point. Can we assume that the unity of all men in an explicit acknowledgement of Christ is a goal to be reached in this historical order? Christians undoubtedly regard such unity in Christ as a hope to be fulfilled in the eschatological order to come. But is it also going to be achieved in an earthly fashion in history? I do not see that this must be so. Since even under the sovereignty of God history is open-ended, offering a manifold of possibilities for actualisation by men, I should not exclude a universal acknowledgement of Christ as impossible in history, though I should regard it as achieved in history as essentially impermanent. Why, however, should we suppose that the elimination of religious plurality within history is an essential part of God's plan and an essential aim for the Christian Church?

Here it is relevant to point to the theme of representation, which runs through the Bible. If one asks concerning the manner of God's acting as manifested in sacred history, then the answer is that the principle of the redemptive process would seem to be the election of a minority for the sake of the whole. It was so with Abraham, called out so that all the nations of the earth should be blessed in him. It was so with Israel as the Chosen People. But this role of representative service was not easily accepted, because it clashed with the drive towards personal and national self-glorification. In the Babylonian Exile, however, after the destruction of the nation as a nation, the theme of representation reached a new height of expression in the Servant figure of the Second-Isaiah, particularly in the Fourth Servant Song, where the sufferings of the Servant, a man of sorrows, are seen as a vicarious atonement for the sins of others. At least one among the meanings of the Servant is that of the true Israel as fulfilling its representative function. Christian tradition, then, sees this function as

9

taken over in a supreme fashion by Jesus Christ. Whatever interpretation is given of the atonement, it cannot fail to regard Christ as having a representative role for mankind.

It would seem reasonable, then, to interpret the mission of the Christian Church in terms of a representative function involving both service and redemptive suffering. Christians will indeed preach Christ universally. Their witness to Christ, when offered without arrogance, will have many indirect effects, apart from direct conversions. And these direct conversions themselves should be regarded, not as the first steps in gathering all men into the Christian Church as a visible community on earth, but as God's election of some for a special representative role. There are many roles, however, in relation to the coming of God's Kingdom. The special role of Christians as forming the community of those who acknowledge Christ should not lead to a denial of the possible roles of men in other religions.

Faith in Christ, therefore, does not, I maintain, imply a denial of the persisting function of other religions in God's ordering of history or of the positive value of religious pluralism.

I hope, however, that the previous exposition has made clear that my granting a positive function to other religions does not mean that I regard all religious traditions as equally true or consider any discussion of the varied contents of these traditions in terms of truth and falsity as out of place. I see no reason for indiscriminately swallowing all that the various religions offer and every reason for engaging in a careful discussion of the difficult issues they raise. Christians will, understandably, evaluate elements from other traditions in the light of Christian criteria. This is perfectly legitimate, provided there is an awareness of one's presuppositions and one is not closed to what another standpoint may offer.

In this regard I should like by way of conclusion to this present investigation as a whole to repudiate the idea that Christians are in an altogether privileged position in regard to knowing the religious situation and understanding other religions. The claim is made in an otherwise open essay by Hans Küng. He writes:

One way in which the Church exists for the sake of the world religions is that she *knows* what the real situation of the world religions is. This is something that the world religions themselves do not know: whence they come, where they now stand, where they are going, what the ultimate situation is between God and man and wherein lies their own true salvation and damnation. The Church can, through her faith, know that her God is also the God of those who belong to the world religions, and that they too come from him and are returning to him; she can know that the one true God has also, in pure grace, made his covenant with mankind in the world religions and that, therefore, Jesus Christ dies and rises again for these men too; so that God's all-powerful mercy shines out also over the nobility and the wretchedness of the world religions. It is only because the Church, in her faith in Jesus Christ, is able to understand the world religions, to know their origin, their course, their goal, their potentialities and limitations, their nature and un-nature, that she is really able to exist for their sake. Hence it is not only a gift to the Church but also a task for her, to see the world religions and understand them for what they really are: to do this in understanding, in openness, in critical freedom and all-embracing goodwill.[9]

This seems to me to confuse God's knowledge of Christ with that possessed by the Church. I find the statement of E. L. Allen in *Christianity Among the Religions* much more balanced. He is speaking of the two forms of Christ, his manifest form among Christians and his latent form among other men. He says:

To neither form of Christ do we have access directly, but in and through historically conditioned religions, of which Christianity is one. We may not therefore assume that as Christians, we possess the key to the understanding of the non-Christian faiths, the criterion by which to distinguish truth from error in them. We know the manifest Christ only in part, so that we are not in a postion to define the outlines of the latent

Christ. The complete Christ, it may be includes a glory in the latent Christ that waits to be recognized and appropriated by those who know him only as manifest.[10]

I should not agree that Christians have no criterion to use in distinguishing truth from error, but they should recognise that any criteria they use depend upon their understanding of Christ, an understanding open to improvement and correction. After all, Christians once used the criterion of Christ to assign all pagans to eternal damnation.

That reminds us how much Christians have already changed their religious conceptions and leads me to conclude with the hope that the meeting of Christians with people of other faiths, the wider ecumenism with which my investigation has been concerned, may result in further reconceptions.

NOTES

NOTES

PART I

1. New York: Scribner's, 1957; 45.
2. Cf. Wilfred Cantwell Smith, "Comparative Religion: Whither—and Why?" in Mircea Eliade and Joseph M. Kitagawa, *eds., The History of Religions: Essays in Methodology* (Chicago: University of Chicago Press, 1959), 31–58.
3. New York: Macmillan, 1967.
4. *World Cultures and World Religions: The Coming Dialogue* (Philadelphia: Westminster Press, 1950), 270.
5. Loc. cit.
6. London: Edinburgh House Press, 1964.
7. Op. cit., 403.
8. *The Yogi and the Devotee* (London: Allen & Unwin, 1968), 14–15.
9. *Reasons and Faiths: An Investigation of Religious Discourse, Christian and Non-Christian* (London: Routledge & Kegan Paul, 1958).
   Doctrine and Argument in Indian Philosophy (London: Allen & Unwin, 1964).
   World Religions: A Dialogue (Harmondsworth: Penguin Books, 1966; 1st ed. 1960).
10. New York: Columbia University Press, 1963; 5.
11. Op. cit., 96.
12. *Asia and Western Dominance.* (New York: Collier Books, 1969), 313.
13. Op. cit., 297.
14. Op. cit., 331.
15. Op. cit., 329.
16. London: Gollancz, 1964.
17. Op. cit., 22.
18. London: Hodder & Stoughton, 1969. See chapter 5 "Light from the East?", 201–35.
19. Op. cit., 235.
20. Arnold J. Toynbee, *Civilization on Trial* (New York: Oxford University Press, 1948), 214–16.
21. *A History of Religion East and West: An Introduction and Interpretation* (London: Macmillan, 1968), 424–5.
22. *The Christian Message in a Non-Christian World*, 3rd ed., 6th printing (Grand Rapids, Michigan: Kregel, 1963), 109.
23. Loc. cit.
24. "Der christliche Glaube and die Weltreligionen", *Gott in Welt: Festgabe für Karl Rahner*, II (Freiburg: Herder, 1964), 291–2.
25. *After Auschwitz: Radical Theology and Contemporary Judaism* (Indianapolis: Bobbs-Merrill, 1966), 263.
26. Ibid., 63.

27. For Radhakrishnan's views, see among his writings: *The Hindu View of Life* (New York: Macmillan, n.d.—from lectures given in 1926); *East and West in Religion* (London: Allen & Unwin, 1958—first edition in 1933); *Eastern Religions and Western Thought* (London: Oxford University Press, 1940; first edition in 1939).

28. *Eastern Religions and Western Thought*, 328.

29. *The Hindu View of Life*, 24.

30. Loc. cit.

31. *The Hindu View of Life*, 27.

32. *Eastern Religions and Western Thought*, 318–19.

33. *The Hindu View of Life*, 37.

34. Ibid., 42.

35. Ibid., 43.

36. *East and West in Religion*, 69–70.

37. Paul David Devanandan, "Renascent Religions and Religion", in Edward J. Jurji, *The Ecumenical Era in Church and Society: A Symposium in Honor of John A. MacKay* (New York: Macmillan, 1959), 169–170.

38. Op. cit., 60.

39. Op. cit., 130.

40. "Radhakrishnan and the Comparative Study of Religion" in *The Philosophy of Sarvepalli Radhakrishnan*, ed. by Paul Arthur Schilpp (New York: Tudor, 1952), 448.

41. Op. cit., 447.

42. *The Hindu View of Life*, 18.

43. Robert Lawson Slater, *World Religions and World Community* (New York: Columbia University Press, 1963), 15–16.

44. Op. cit., 84.

45. *Rg Veda* i. 164.46.

46. New York: Scribner's, 1955; 58.

47. See *The Yogi and the Devotee*, chapter IV "The Thesis of Religious Unity".

48. Scriptural quotations are from *The Jerusalem Bible* (London: Darton, Longman & Todd, 1966).

49. "The World Religions in God's Plan of Salvation" in *Christian Revelation and World Religions*, edited by Joseph Neuner, S.J. (London: Burns Oates, 1967), 31 ff.

50. For a history of the question, see Louis Capéran, *Le Problème de salut des infidèles: Essai historique* (Toulouse: Grand Seminaire, 1934); or, more briefly, Yves Congar, O.P., *The Wide World My Parish* (London: Darton, Longman & Todd, 1961), chapter 10 "No Salvation Outside the Church", 93–154. For a recent theological account, which draws upon the writings of Karl Rahner, see Anita Röper, *The Anonymous Christian* (New York: Sheed & Ward, 1966)—the book includes an essay by Klaus Riesenhuber, S.J., "The Anonymous Christian According to Karl Rahner"; for an earlier brief essay of my own see "Can Unbelievers Be Saved?" in *The Study of Theology*

(London, Sheed & Ward, 1962; American edition, *Theology For Today*, New York: Sheed & Ward, 1962), chapter 8.

51. See the text of the Constitution nos. 13–17. An English translation is to be found in *The Documents of Vatican II* edited by Walter M. Abbott, S.J. and Joseph Gallagher (London: Geoffrey Chapman, 1966).

52. See *Church Dogmatics, Volume I The Doctrine of the Word of God,* 2nd half-volume, edited by G. W. Bromiley and T. F. Torrance (Edinburgh: T. & T. Clark, 1956), section 17 "The Revelation of God as the Abolition of Religion", 280–361.

53. Loc. cit., 325.

54. Loc. cit., 327. Author's italics.

55. Loc. cit., 338.

56. Loc. cit., 344.

57. Among Brunner's writings see especially *Revelation and Reason: The Christian Doctrine of Faith and Knowledge* (Philadelphia: Westminster Press, 1946).

58. New York: Harper.

59. In Leroy S. Rouner, ed. *Philosophy, Religion and the Coming World Civilization: Essays in Honor of William Ernest Hocking* (The Hague: Martinus Nijhoff, 1966), 230.

60. *Religion and the Christian Faith* (London: Lutterworth, 1961, 1st ed. 1956), *World Cultures and World Religions: The Coming Dialogue* (Philadelphia: Westminster Press, 1960), *Why Christianity of All Religions?* (London: Lutterworth, 1962).

61. "Das Christentum und die nichtchristlichen Religionen", *Schriften zur Theologie* V (Einsiedeln, 1964), 136–158.

62. "Der christliche Glaube und die Weltreligionen", in *Gott in Welt: Festgabe für Karl Rahner II* (Freiburg: Herder, 1964), 287–305.

63. *Die Religionen als Thema der Theologie* (Freiburg: Herder, 1963); Eng. trans. *Towards a Theology of Religions* (Freiburg: Herder & London: Burns Oates, 1966). Id., "Einige Thesen zum Selbstverständnis der Theologie angesichts der Religionen" in *Gott in Welt: Festgabe für Karl Rahner* II (Freiburg: Herder, 1964), 306–316.

64. "Die ausserbiblische Menschheit und die Weltreligionen" in *Mysterium Salutis: Grundriss heilsgeschichtlicher Dogmatik,* hrsg. van Johannes Feiner und Magnus Löhrer (Einsiedeln: Benzinger) II (1967), 1049–1075.

65. "The World Religions in God's Plan of Salvation" in *Christian Revelation and World Religions,* ed. by Joseph Neuner, S.J. (London: Burns & Oates, 1967), 25–66.

66. *The Documents of Vatican II,* edited by Walter M. Abbott, S.J., and Joseph Gallagher (London: Geoffrey Chapman, 1966), 662–3.

67. Quoted in E. C. Dewick, *The Christian Attitude to Other Religions* (Cambridge: University Press, 1963), 50.

68. An historical account of these attitudes is given in E. L. Allen, *Christianity Among the Religions* (London: Allen & Unwin, 1960). A useful collection of texts from the modern period with brief introductions

and an initial essay is given in Owen C. Thomas, *Attitudes Toward Other Religions; Some Christian Interpretations* (London: SCM Press, 1969).

69. Op. cit., 10.
70. See H. Richard Niebuhr, *Christ and Culture* (New York: Harper, 1956; 1st ed. 1951).
71. Op. cit., 43–44.
72. *Foolishness to the Greeks: An Inaugural Lecture delivered before the University of Oxford on 2 November 1953* (Oxford: Clarendon Press, 1953), 17. Author's italics.
73. London: Oxford University Press, 5th impression, 1939; first published in 1913.
74. Op. cit., 145.
75. Op. cit., 146–7.
76. Niebuhr, op. cit., 147.
77. Op. cit., 194.
78. "The Relation of Christians to their Non-Christian Surroundings", *Christian Revelation and World Religions*, Neuner, S.J. (London: Burns & Oates, 1967), 168–9. Author's italics.
79. "Some Similarities and Differences Between Christianity and Islam: An Essay in Comparative Religion" in *The World of Islam. Studies in Honour of Philip K. Hitti,* edited by James Kritzeck and R. Bayly Winder (London: Macmillan, 1960), 49.
80. On the question of Christianity and religious conservatism, see Joseph Ratzinger, "Der christliche Glaube und die Weltreligionen" in *Gott in Welt: Festgabe für Karl Rahner* II (Freiburg: Herder, 1964), 290.

PART II

1. *What World Religions Teach.* 2nd ed. enlarged. (London: Harrap, 1968), 192.
2. "On Understanding Non-Christian Religions" in *The History of Religions: Essays in Methodology*, edited by Mircea Eliade and Joseph M. Kitagawa (Chicago: University of Chicago Press, 1959), 131.
3. *The Faith of Other Men* (New York: New American Library, 1963), 91–2.
4. New York: New American Library, 1964.
5. Op. cit., 16.
6. Op. cit., 175.
7. Op. cit., 172.
8. Cf. Winston L. King, *A Thousand Lives Away: Buddhism in Contemporary Burma* (Cambridge, Massachusetts: Harvard University Press, 1964).
9. R. H. L. Slater, "Religious Diversity and Religious Reconception" in *Philosophy, Religion and the Coming World Civilization: Essays in*

Honor of William Ernest Hocking, edited by Leroy S. Rouner (The Hague: Martinus Nijhoff, 1966), 261–2. Author's italics.

10. For a moderate but effective critique of the book, see E. H. Pyle, "In Defence of 'Religion'", *Religious Studies* 3 (1967), 347–353. The strictures of Kees W. Bolle in his review in *The Journal of Religion* 44 (1964), 170–2, seem to me excessive and one-sided.

11. Op. cit., 158–60.

12. For a view of the Church as a social movement without a clearly defined membership, see the Roman Catholic theologian, Gregory Baum in his book, *The Credibility of the Church Today: A Reply to Charles Davis* (New York: Herder and Herder, 1968), 196 ff.

13. See his *Dynamics of Faith* (New York: Harper Torchbooks, 1958).

14. Cf. *Ultimate Concern: Tillich in Dialogue*, edited by D. MacKenzie Brown (London: SCM Press, 1965), 11.

15. For the psychological importance of this, see Erich Fromm, *The Art of Loving* (New York: Bantam Books, 1963), 99–101.

16. I have taken this idea from an unpublished paper of Bernard Lonergan, S.J., "The Future of Christianity".

17. "The History of Religions as a Preparation for the Co-operation of Religions" in *The History of Religions: Essays in Methodology*, edited by Mircea Eliade and Joseph M. Kitagawa (Chicago: University of Chicago Press, 1959), 132–160, especially 142–53.

18. *An Historian's Approach to Religion* (London: Oxford University Press, 1956), 262–285.

19. Cf. R. C. Zaehner's remarks on Toynbee in the Conclusion he wrote as Editor in *The Concise Encyclopaedia of Living Faiths* (London: Hutchinson, 1959), 413–17.

20. Cf. the heading of Toynbee's chapter in the work cited: "The Task of Disengaging the Essence from the Non-essentials in Mankind's Religious Heritage".

21. See his *Mysticism Sacred and Profane* (London: Oxford University Press, Galaxy Book, 1967; first published 1957) and *Hindu and Muslim Mysticism* (New York: Schocken Books, 1969; first published 1960). His theory of mysticism is an important theme in his more general writings, namely: *The Comparison of Religions* (Boston: Beacon Press, 1962; originally published as *At Sunday Times*, London: Faber, 1958); *The Convergent Spirit: Towards a Dialectics of Religion* (London: Routledge and Kegan Paul, 1963); *The Catholic Church and World Religions* (London: Burns & Oates, 1964).

22. *Mysticism Sacred and Profane*, 204.

23. Cf. 150–2.

24. *The Yogi and the Devotee*, 66–75.

25. *Revelation and Religion: Studies in the Theological Interpretation of Religious Types* (London: Nisbet, 1954).

26. Op. cit., 164.

27. Cf. Ninian Smart, *Doctrine and Argument in Indian Philosophy* (London: Allen & Unwin, 1964), 36–8.

28. Winston L. King, *Buddhism and Christianity: Some Bridges of Under-standing* (Philadelphia: Westminster, 1962), 205.
29. Op. cit., 37.
30. *The Idea of the Holy*, trans. by John W. Harvey, fifth impression revised with additions (London: Oxford University Press, 1928), 39.
31. H. D. Lewis and Robert Lawson Slater, *World Religions: Meeting Points and Major Issues* (London: Watts, 1966), 159–69.
32. Op. cit., 168–9.
33. Op. cit., 204–27.
34. Op. cit., 227. Author's italics.

PART III

1. Cf. for example, Wilfred Cantwell Smith in "Some Similarities and Differences Between Christianity and Islam: An Essay in Comparative Religion", *The World of Islam: Studies in Honour of Philip K. Hitti*, edited by James Kritzeck and R. Bayly Winder (London: Macmillan, 1960), 47–59.
2. *Order and History. Volume One: Israel and Revelation* (Louisiana State University Press, 1956). See, in particular, chapter 11 "The Deuteronomic Torah".
3. Op. cit., chapter 4, "Israel and History".
4. Cf. *Systematic Theology I* (Digwell Place, Welwyn: Nisbet, 1964), 112–17. The context and implications of the phrase in Tillich are different from mine.
5. For an essay linking Aquinas's treatment to modern psychology see Victor White, O.P., *God and the Unconscious* (London: Harvill Press, 1952), chapter VII: "Revelation and the Unconscious".
6. *Christ and Culture*, 14.
7. Cf. *The Foundations of New Testament Christology* (London: Lutterworth, 1965), 130–1.
8. For a vigorous critique of the traditional thesis of the necessity of the Church by a Roman Catholic theologian, see Richard P. McBrien, *Do We Need the Church?* (London: Collins, 1969).
9. Hans Küng, "The World Religions in God's Plan of Salvation" in Joseph Neuner, ed., *Christian Revelation and World Religions* (London: Burns & Oates, 1967), 59–60. Author's italics.
10. E. L. Allen, *Christianity Among the Religions* (London: Allen & Unwin, 1960), 155.

LIST OF BOOKS

LIST OF BOOKS

This is not a complete bibliography of the subject, but a list of the writings I have used in the immediate preparation of this book.

Bertil Albrektson, *History and the Gods: An Essay on the Role of Historical Events as Divine Manifestations in the Ancient Near East and Israel.* Coniectanea Biblica, Old Testament Series, 1 (Lund: CWK Gleerup, 1907).

E. L. Allen, *Christianity among the Religions* (London: Allen & Unwin, 1960).

Philip H. Ashby, *The Conflict of Religions* (New York: Scribner's, 1958).

Peter R. Baelz, *Christian Theology and Metaphysics* (Philadelphia: Fortess Press, 1968).

Karl Barth, *Church Dogmatics. Volume I, The Doctrine of the Word of God,* 2nd half volume, edited by G. W. Bromley and T. F. Torrance (Edinburgh: T. & T. Clark, 1956). Section 17, "The Revelation of God as the abolition of Religion", 280–361.

Gregory Baum, *The Credibility of the Church Today: A Reply to Charles Davis* (New York: Herder and Herder, 1968).

Gregory Baum, "Christianity and Other Religions: A Catholic Problem", *Cross Currents* 16 (1966), 447–162.

Ernst Benz and Minoru Nambara, *Das Christentum und die nicht-christlichen Hochreligionen: Begegnung und Auseinandersetzung: Eine internationale Bibliographie.* Beihefte der Zeitschrift für Religions- und Geistesgeschichte, 5 (Leiden: Brill, 1960).

Ernst Benz, "On Understanding Non-Christian Religions" in Mircea Eliade and Joseph M. Kitagawa, eds., *The History of Religions: Essays in Methodology* (Chicago: University of Chicago Press, 1959), 113-31.

C. J. Bleeker, *Christ in Modern Athens: The Confrontation of Christianity with Modern Culture and the Non-Christian Religions* (Leiden: Brill, 1963).

Kees W. Bolle, *The Persistence of Religion: An Essay on Tantrism and Sri Aurobindo's Philosophy.* With a Preface by Mircea Eliade. Studies in the History of Religions: Supplements to *Numen*, VIII (Leiden: Brill, 1965).

A. C. Bouquet, *The Christian Religion and its Competitors Today: Being the Hulsean Lectures for 1924–5 Delivered Before the University of Cambridge* (Cambridge: University Press, 1925).

A. C. Bouquet, *Is Christianity the Final Religion? a Candid Enquiry with the Materials for an Opinion* (London: Macmillan, 1921).

Emil, Brunner, *Revolution and Reason: The Christian Doctrine of Faith and Knowledge*. Trans. by Olive Wyon. (Philadelphia: Westminster Press, 1916).

Louis Capéran, *Le Problème du salut des infidèles: Essai historique*. Nouvelle édition, revue et mise à jour (Toulouse: Grand Séminaire, 1934).

Louis Capéran, *Le Problème du salut des infidèles: Essai théologique*. Nouvelle édition, revue et mise à jour (Toulouse: Grand Séminaire, 1934).

Yves Congar, O. P., *The Wide World My Parish: Salvation and Its Problems* (London: Darton, Longman & Todd, 1961).

Étienne Cornelis, O. P., *Valeurs chrétiennes des religions non-chrétiennes: Histoire du salut et histoire des religions: Christianisme et Bouddhisme* (Paris: Cerf, 1965).

Kenneth Cragg, *Christianity in World Perspective* (London: Lutterworth, 1968).

Jacques-Albert Cuttat, *La rencontre des religions: avec une étude sur la spiritualité de l'Orient chrétien*. Les religions, 12 (Paris: Aubier, 1957).

Paul David Devanandan, "Renascent Religions and Religion" in Edward J. Jurji, *The Ecumenical Era in Church and Society: A Symposium in Honor of John A. MacKay* (New York: Macmillan, 1959), 148-76.

E. C. Dewick, *The Christian Attitude to Other Religions* (Cambridge: University Press, 1953).

David L. Edwards, *Religion and Change*. Twentieth Century Studies (London: Hodder and Stoughton, 1969).

Herbert H. Farmer, *Revelation and Religion: Studies in the Theological Interpretation of Religious Types* (London: Nisbet, 1954).

W. R. Farmer, C. F. D. Moule & R. R. Niebuhr, *eds., Christian History and Interpretation: Studies Presented to John Knox* (Cambridge: University Press, 1967).

J. N. Farquhar, *The Crown of Hinduism*. Fifth impression (London: Oxford University Press, 1930).

The Finality of Jesus Christ in the Age of Universal History. Bulletin: Division of Studies of World Council of Churches. VIII, 2, 1962.

Walter Freytag, *The Gospel and the Religions: A Biblical Enquiry*. I.M.C. Research Pamphlets, no. 5 (London: SCM Press, 1957).

Erich Fromm, *The Art of Loving* (New York: Bantam Books, 1963).

Reginald H. Fuller, *The Foundations of New Testament Christology* (London: Lutterworth, 1965).

Friedrich Heiler, "The History of Religions as a Preparation for the

Co-operation of Religions" in Mircea Eliade and Joseph M. Kitagawa, *eds., The History of Religions: Essays in Methodology* (Chicago: University of Chicago Press, 1959), 132–160.

William Ernest Hocking, *Living Religions and a World Faith* (London: Allen & Unwin, 1940).

A. G. Hogg, "Towards Clarifying my Reactions to Dr Kraemer's Book", *International Missionary Council*. 4th Meeting. Madras, 1938, Volume I.

Walter Horton, "Tambaram Twenty-Five Years After" in Leroy S. Rouner, *ed.: Philosophy, Religion and the Coming World Civilization: Essays in Honor of William Ernest Hocking* (The Hague: Martinus Nijhoff, 1966), 225–234.

E. O. James, *Christianity and Other Religions*. Knowing Christianity. (London: Hodder and Stoughton, 1968).

Winston L. King, *Buddhism and Christianity: Some Bridges of Understanding* (Philadelphia: Westminster Press, 1962).

Winston L. King, *Introduction to Religion: A Phenomenological Approach*. Revised edition (New York: Harper, 1968).

Winston L. King, *A Thousand Lives Away: Buddhism in Contemporary Burma* (Cambridge, Massachusetts: Harvard University Press, 1964).

Hendrik Kraemer, *The Christian Message in a Non-Christian World*, 3rd ed., 6th printing (Grand Rapids, Michigan: Kregel, 1963).

Hendrik Kraemer, *Religion and the Christian Faith* (London: Lutterworth, 1961).

Hendrik Kraemer, *World Cultures and World Religions: The Coming Dialogue* (Philadelphia: Westminster Press, 1960).

Hendrik Kraemer, *Why Christianity of All Religions?* (London: Lutterworth, 1962).

Hendrik Kraemer, "The encounter between East and West in the civilization of our time" in Edward J. Jurji, *The Ecumenical Era in Church and Society: a Symposium in Honor of John A. Mackay* (New York: The Macmillan Company, 1959), 92–107.

Hendrik Kraemer, "The Role and Responsibility of the Christian Mission" in Leroy S. Rouner, *ed., Philosophy, Religion and the Coming World Civilization: Essays in Honor of William Ernest Hocking* (The Hague: Martinus Nijhoff, 1966), 235–249.

H. D. Lewis and Robert Lawson Slater, *World Religions: Meeting Points and Major Issues*, The New Thinker's Library (London: Watts, 1966).

Trevor Ling, *Buddha, Marx and God: Some Aspects of Religion in the Modern World* (London: Macmillan, 1966).

Trevor Ling, *A History of Religion East and West: An Introduction and Interpretation* (London: Macmillan, 1968).

10

Trevor Ling, *Prophetic Religion* (London: Macmillan, 1966).

Thomas Luckmann, *The Invisible Religion: The Problem of Religion in Modern Society* (New York: Macmillan, 1967).

Richard P. McBrien, *Do We Need the Church?* (London: Collins, 1969).

David W. McKain, *Christianity: Some Non-Christian Appraisals.* With an Introduction by Robert Lawson Slater (New York: McGraw Hill, 1964).

Guy S. Métraux and François Crouzet, *eds., Religions and the Promise of the Twentieth Century* (New York: Mentor Book, New American Library, 1965).

Nicol MacNicol, *Is Christianity Unique? A Comparative Study of the Religions* (Wilde Lectures, Oxford, 1935).

C. F. D. Moule, "Is Christ Unique?" in C. F. D. Moule and others, *Faith, Fact and Fantasy* (London: Collins, Fontana Books, 1964).

Peter Munz, *Problems of Religious Knowledge* (London: SCM Press, 1959).

Stephen Neill, *Christian Faith and Other Faiths: The Christian Dialogue with Other Religions* (London: Oxford University Press, 1961).

Joseph Neuner, S.J., *ed., Christian Revelation and World Religions.* Compass Books (London: Burns & Oates, 1967).

Leslie Newbigin, *The Finality of Christ* (London: SCM Press, 1969).

H. Richard Niebuhr, *Christ and Culture* (New York: Harper, 1951).

Rudolf Otto, *The Idea of the Holy.* Translated by John W. Harvey. Fifth impression revised with additions (London: Oxford University Press, 1928).

K. M. Panikkar, *Asia and Western Dominance* (New York: Collier Books, 1969).

Raymond Panikkar, *The Unknown Christ of Hinduism* (London: Darton, Longman & Todd, 1961).

Geoffrey Parrinder, *The Christian Debate: Light from the East* (London: Gollancz, 1964).

Geoffrey Parrinder, *What World Religions Teach*, 2nd ed. enlarged (London: Harrap, 1968).

Eric H. Pyle, "Diagnoses of Religion", in F. G. Healey, *ed., Prospect for Theology: Essays in Honour of H. H. Farmer* (Digswell Place, Welwyn: Nisbet, 1966).

Eric H. Pyle, "In Defence of 'Religion' ", *Religious Studies*, 3 (1967), 347–353.

S. Radhakrishnan, *East and West in Religion.* 4th Impression (London: Allen & Unwin, 1958).

S. Radhakrishnan, *Eastern Religions and Western Thought.* 2nd ed. (London: Oxford University Press, 1940).

S. Radhakrishnan, *Fellowship of the Spirit* (Cambridge, Massachusetts: Center for the Study of World Religions, Harvard, 1961).

S. Radhakrishnan, *The Hindu View of Life* (New York: Macmillan, n.d.).

S. Radhakrishnan, *Kalki or The Future of Civilization.* 4th ed. (Bombay: Hind Kitabs, 1956).

Karl Rahner, "Das Christentum und die nichtchristlichen Religionen" in *Schriften zur Theologie* V (Einsiedeln, 1964), 136–158.

Joseph Ratzinger, "Der christliche Glaube und die Weltreligionen", *Gott in Welt: Festgabe für Karl Rahner*, II (Freiburg: Herder, 1964), 287–303.

Re-Thinking Missions: A Laymen's Inquiry after one hundred years. By the Commission of Appraisal, William Ernest Hocking, Chairman (New York: Harper, 1932).

Anita Röper, *The Anonymous Christian*, trans. by Joseph Donceel, S.J. With an Afterword, The Anonymous Christian According to Karl Rahner by Klaus Riesenhuber, S.J. (New York: Sheed & Ward, 1966).

Richard L. Rubenstein, *After Auschwitz: Radical Theology and Contemporary Judaism* (Indianapolis: Bobbs-Merrill, 1966).

D. S. Sarma, *Renascent Hinduism* (Bombay: Bharatiya Vidya Bhavan, 1966).

Heinz Robert Schlette, "Einige Thesen zum Selbstverstandnis der Theologie angesichts der Religionen", in *Gott in Welt: Festgabe für Karl Rahner*, II (Freiburg: Herder, 1964), 306–316.

Heinz Robert Schlette, *Epiphany as History* (London: Sheed and Ward, 1969).

Heinz Robert Schlette, *Towards a Theology of Religions.* Quaestiones Disputatae 14 (Freiburg: Herder & London: Burns & Oates, 1966).

Albert Schweitzer, *Christianity and the Religions of the World* (New York: Holt, 1939).

Roger Lincoln Shinn, *Christianity and the Problem of History* (St. Louis: Abbott, 1964).

Robert Lawson Slater, *Can Christians Learn From Other Religions?* (New York: Seabury Press, 1963).

Robert Lawson Slater, "Religious Diversity and Religious Reconception" in Leroy S. Rouner, *ed.*, *Philosophy, Religion and the Coming World Civilization: Essays in Honor of William Ernest Hocking* (The Hague: Martinus Nijhoff, 1966), 250–262.

Robert Lawson Slater, *World Religions and World Community* (New York: Columbia University Press, 1963).

Ninian Smart, *Doctrine and Argument in Indian Philosophy*, Muirhead Library of Philosophy (London: Allen and Unwin, 1964).

Ninian Smart, *Reasons and Faiths: An Investigation of Religious Dis-*

course, Christian and Non-Christian (London: Routledge & Kegan Paul, 1958).

Ninian Smart, *The Yogi and the Devotee: The Interplay between the Upanishads and Catholic Theology* (London: George Allen & Unwin, 1968).

Ninian Smart, *World Religions: A Dialogue* (Harmondsworth, Middlesex: Penguin, 1966; first published 1960).

Ninian Smart, "The Relation Between Christianity and the Other Great Religions" in *Soundings: Essays Concerning Christian Understanding*, ed. by A. R. Vidler (Cambridge: University Press, 1962), 103–121.

Wilfred Cantwell Smith, *The Faith of Other Men* (New York: New American Library, 1963).

Wilfred Cantwell Smith, *Islam in Modern History*. A Mentor Book (New York: New American Library, 1963).

Wilfred Cantwell Smith, *The Meaning and End of Religion: A New Approach to the Religious Traditions of Mankind*. A Mentor Book (New York: New American Library, 1964).

Wilfred Cantwell Smith, *Questions of Religious Truth* (New York: Scribner, 1967).

Wilfred Cantwell Smith, "Comparative Religion: Whither—and Why?" in Mircea Eliade and Joseph M. Kitagawa, *eds.*, *The History of Religions: Essays in Methodology* (Chicago: University of Chicago Press, 1959), 31–58.

Wilfred Cantwell Smith, "Some Similarities and Differences Between Christianity and Islam: An Essay in Comparative Religion" in *The World of Islam: Studies in Honour of Philip K. Hitti*, ed. by James Kritzeck and R. Bayly Winder (London: Macmillan, 1960), 47–59.

W. Taylor Stevenson, *History as Myth: The Import for Contemporary Theology* (New York: The Seabury Press, 1969).

Bernhard Stoeckle, "Die ausserbiblishche Menschheit und die Weltreligionen" in *Mysterium Salutis: Grundriss heilsgechichtlicher Dogmatik*, hrsg. von Johannes Feiner und Magnus Löhrer (Einsideln: Benzinger) II (1967), 1049–1075.

John V. Taylor, *The Primal Vision: Christian Presence amid African Religion* (London: SCM Press, 1963).

Gustave Thils, *Syncrétisme ou Catholicité?* (Tournai: Casterman, 1967).

Owen C. Thomas, *ed.*, *Attitudes Towards Other Religions: Some Christian Interpretations*. Forum Books (London: SCM Press, 1969).

Paul Tillich, *Christianity and the Encounter of the World Religions* (New York: Columbia University Press, 1963).

Paul Tillich, *Dynamics of Faith* (New York: Harper Torchbooks, 1958).

Paul Tillich, *The Future of Religions* (New York: Harper, 1966).

Paul Tillich, *Systematic Theology* 3v. (Digswell Place, Welwyn: Nisbet, 1964).

Paul Tillich, *Ultimate Concern: Tillich in Dialogue*, edited by D. McKenzie Brown (London: SCM Press, 1965).

Arnold Toynbee, *An Historian's Approach to Religion* (London: Oxford University Press, 1956).

Arnold Toynbee, *Christianity Among the Religions of the World* (New York: Scribner, 1957).

Arnold Toynbee, *Civilization on Trial* (New York: Oxford University Press, 1948).

Arend Th. Van Leeuwen, *Christianity in World History: The Meeting of the Faiths of East and West.* Foreword by Dr. Hendrik Kraemer (London: Edinburgh House Press, 1964).

H. Van Straelen, S.V.D., *The Catholic Encounter with World Religions* (London: Burns & Oates, 1966).

Joachim Wach, "Radhakrishnan and the Comparative Study of Religion" in *The Philosophy of Sarvepalli Radhakrishnan*, ed. by Paul Arthur Schilpp (New York: Tudor, 1952), 443–458.

William Montgomery Watt, *Truth in the Religions: A Sociological and Psychological Approach* (Edinburgh: University Press, n.d.).

Victor White, O.P., *God and the Unconscious* (London: Harvill, 1952).

R. C. Zaehner, *The Catholic Church and World Religions.* Faith and Fact Books, 140 (London: Burns & Oates, 1964).

R. C. Zaehner, *The Comparison of Religions.* With a new preface by the author (Boston: Beacon Press, 1962).

R. C. Zaehner, ed., *The Concise Encyclopaedia of Living Faiths* (London: Hutchinson, 1959).

R. C. Zaehner, *The Convergent Spirit: Towards a Dialectic of Religion.* Religious Perspectives, 8 (London: Routledge & Kegan Paul, 1963).

R. C. Zaehner, *Foolishness to the Greeks: An Inaugural Lecture delivered before the University of Oxford on 2 November 1953* (Oxford: Clarendon Press, 1953).

R. C. Zaehner, *Hindu and Muslim Mysticism* (New York: Schocken Books, 1969).

R. C. Zaehner, *Mysticism: Sacred and Profane: An Inquiry into Some Varieties of Praeternatural Experience* (London: Oxford University Press. Galaxy Book, 1967; first published 1957).

INDEX

INDEX

Abraham, 129
Absolute, religious concept of, 31–32, 86, 88, 93, 106
adjectival religion, 92
Advaita Vedanta, 35, 36, 105, 107
Allen, E. L., 131–132
Amitabha, 106
Anatman, doctrine of, 95
Anglican attitude to other religions, 48, 52
Aquinas, St. Thomas, 52
Arjuna, 122
Arnold, Sir Edwin, 18
Ashby, Philip H., 38
Atman (Brahman Atman), 105
Auschwitz Concentration Camp, 29
authenticity (human), 77–78, 80–81

Babylonian Exile, 129
Barth, Karl, 44–46
Beatles, The, 19
Benz, Ernst, 63
Bhagavad-Gita, 105, 122
bhakti (contemplation), 90
Bible, its position in Christianity, 104, 116; *see* also New Testament and Old Testament
Bodhisattvas, 106
Brunner, Emil, 44, 46

Buddhism, 16, 17, 18, 19, 21, 23, 26, 29, 57, 65–68, 69–70, 71, 72, 87, 91, 93–97, 102, 106–107, 112, 115, 116; *see* also Mahayana Buddhism, Theravada Buddhism and Zen Buddhism
Buddhism and Christianity, quoted, 96
Bultmann, Rudolf, 125
Burma, primitive Buddhism in, 67, 96

Catholicism, 41, 42–43, 44, 47–48, 52, 53, 54, 72, 84, 90, 104
Chicago World Fair (1893), 18
China, 18, 27, 69, 72
Christ (Christianity), 13–18, 19–22, 23–29, 34, 35, 37–38, 39–60, 63–73, 84–92, 94, 96, 102, 103–104, 112, 115, 116, 118–132
Christ and Culture, quoted, 53–54
Christianity Among the Religions of the World, quoted, 14, 131
Christianity and the Encounter of the World Religions, quoted, 22
Christianity in World History: The Meeting of the Faiths of East and West, quoted, 20–21
Christology, 39–40, 124–126
Civilization on Trial, 24

BIBLICAL REFERENCES